Natural Resources

AND THE

Great Depression

IN MARTIN COUNTY AND SOUTH-CENTRAL INDIANA

The Memoirs of William B. Barnes, Sr.

INDIANA HISTORICAL COLLECTIONS
VOLUME 56

ISSN 0073-6880
ISBN 1-885323-56-5

Natural Resources
AND THE
Great Depression
IN MARTIN COUNTY AND SOUTH-CENTRAL INDIANA

The Memoirs of William B. Barnes, Sr.

Edited by

WEINTRAUT & ASSOCIATES
HISTORIANS, INC.

INDIANA HISTORICAL BUREAU
INDIANAPOLIS 2005

Photograph opposite page: Bill Barnes beside a black oak in the research natural area in the Hoosier National Forest.

ISSN 0073-6880
ISBN 1-885323-56-5
Library of Congress Control Number: 2005928502

The paper used in this publication meets the minimum requirements of the American National Standard for Informational Sciences–Permanence of Paper for Printed Library Materials, ANSI Z39.48-1994

This book is dedicated to past and present generations of Hoosiers, who have practiced the conservation and wise use of our natural resources in order for future generations to enjoy, manage and protect them from unwise utilization.

TABLE OF CONTENTS

MAPS

PREFACE AND ACKNOWLEDGEMENTS

Preface

This book focuses on the conditions of the natural resources and economy during the Great Depression in Martin County and south-central Indiana. Martin County is a good example of the conditions that existed in southern Indiana during the Great Depression. Past uses and abuses of natural resources greatly affected the economy of this county. Remedial measures were initiated during the 1930s by various state and federal agencies involved in conservation work. The U.S. Department of Agriculture acquired the area in Martin County later known as the White River Land Utilization Project, and the Resettlement Administration removed and resettled the people living on this submarginal farming land. Federal policies were used to develop and convert the area for forestry and recreational purposes. The Indiana Department of Conservation, Division of Forestry agreed to manage the area as a state forest under a ninety-nine year lease with the federal government. However, the lease was soon cancelled in late 1940, when the U.S. Navy selected the area for a major inland ammunition storage depot in preparation for World War II.

The various military functions of the facility remained during the ensuing Cold War period and continue to the present day. The aftermath of all these changes has resulted in Crane Division, Naval Surface Warfare Center being one of the largest employers in southern Indiana. Ultimately, this conversion of land use in

BIOGRAPHY OF
WILLIAM B. BARNES, SR.

William Bryan Barnes was born November 3, 1908, and was named after the famous orator and presidential candidate, William Jennings Bryan. He grew up on the Eastern Shore in Seaford, Delaware, and developed a love of nature at an early age on hunting and fishing trips with his father, who was a section foreman on a branch line of the Pennsylvania Railroad. Much of his childhood was spent in fishing the old millpond near his home.

After graduating from high school in 1926, he attended Pennsylvania State Forest School in Mont Alto, which, at that time, was the oldest forestry school in Pennsylvania. In 1929, the school was consolidated with Pennsylvania State College (now University). His junior class and the two lower classes were given the option of transferring to Pennsylvania State or elsewhere. He and most of the three classes transferred to North Carolina State University. He graduated from North Carolina in 1930.

After a three-year stint with the Florida Forest Service, the author came to Indiana in 1933 as a camp forester with the Civilian Conservation Corps at Jasper. He transferred in 1935 to the U.S. Department of Agriculture and Resettlement Administration project, which is now part of the Crane Division,

Naval Surface Warfare Center. While with the Resettlement Administration, he met and married Cecilia R. Doyle in 1938 at Loogootee. In 1940, they moved to Indianapolis, where they resided until his retirement in 1977.

Thus, on July 1, 1940, he began his thirty-seven-year career with the Indiana Department of Conservation, which became the Department of Natural Resources. Most of this time was spent as Federal Aid Coordinator allocating funds from the Pittman-Robertson and Dingell-Johnson programs for the fish and wildlife areas around the state. His last ten years were spent as the first director of the Division of Nature Preserves, which continues to set aside some of the best remaining forest and prairie habitats in the state.

He received many awards and accolades during his employment. On October 29, 1987, the Indiana Natural Resources Commission dedicated the Bill Barnes Nature Preserve located in Newton County on the Willow Slough State Fish and Wildlife Area.

Barnes has been active in birding and is a past president of the Indiana Audubon Society. Other interests include gardening and other outdoor pursuits. He still enjoys getting out with his sons—watching the spring migration of waterfowl in South Dakota with Bill Jr., walking through prairie flowers and trees in Wisconsin with John, or watching the sun set over the Pacific in Hawaii with Phil.

He currently resides in Huron, South Dakota. His three sons all continue to protect and enhance the wildlife legacy he taught us.

—William B. Barnes, Jr.

FOREWORD:
A CONSERVATION LEGACY

It is not often that one has the opportunity to write a foreword to a book whose author spent forty-four years protecting the state's natural resources. William B. Barnes is such an author.

Bill Barnes spent the years of the Great Depression working on New Deal programs in Indiana. Following two years as camp forester with the Civilian Conservation Corps, Bill served as chief forester with the U.S. Department of Agriculture and Resettlement Administration in Martin County in the last years of the 1930s. He was part of an effort to create a state forest on submarginal farmland, that later became the Crane Division, Naval Surface Warfare Center. On July 1, 1940, Bill began thirty-seven years with the Indiana Department of Natural Resources (then Indiana Department of Conservation), first as Federal Aid Coordinator for the Division of Fish and Game, later as assistant director of the division. During most of his last decade of state employment, Bill distinguished himself as director of the Division of Nature Preserves of IDNR and retired at age sixty-eight.

The Indiana Nature Preserves Act of 1967 specifies that lands dedicated as State Nature Preserves serve "the highest and best use" of any tracts within the state. Bill Barnes and his successors rigorously followed this tenet. The finest of Indiana natural lands have been chosen as state nature preserves and, once dedicated, the protected status of these nature preserves has never been challenged.

Bill Barnes is justifiably proud of the continuing success of the Indiana Division of Nature Preserves Program that he initiated and carefully shepherded during its formative years. As a living legacy for the citizens of Indiana, the number of nature preserves recently reached 200 with a total of 28,460 acres. This milestone was observed at a meeting in November 2003 of the Indiana Natural Resources Commission, when Kramer Woods, a remnant of pre-settlement forest of exceptional quality in Spencer County, was dedicated.

Bill's memberships, honors, and awards during his long and effective years of service are many and well deserved. Included are: a Charter Member of The Wildlife Society, both the national and Indiana chapters; and memberships in the Indiana Academy of Science, the Indiana Chapter of The Nature Conservancy, Wilderness Society, Indiana Audubon Society, ACRES, Inc., and the Indiana Conservation and Outdoor Education Association. He has held chairmanships of the National Flyway Council, Mississippi Flyway Council, and the Preservation of the Natural Areas Committee (IAS). He also served as president of the Indiana Audubon Society, and the Midwest Association of Fish, Game, and Conservation Commission. For many years, Bill and his wife Cecilia both served on the board of trustees of the Indiana Chapter of The Nature Conservancy.

Bill has received the Charles S. Osborne Award in Wildlife Conservation granted by Purdue University; the Hoosier Award of the Indiana Chapter of the Wildlife Society for outstanding contributions to the profession of Wildlife Management; Environmental Quality Award, U.S. EPA; Earl Brooks Award in Conservation of Natural Resources from the Indiana Audubon Society; National Oak Leaf Award from The Nature Conservancy; Presidential Citation, Indiana Chapter of the National Wildlife Federation; Outstanding Contribution to Conservation of Natural Resources of Indiana, by the Indiana Conservation Council, Inc.; George B. Fell Award from the Natural Areas Association; and Sagamore of the Wabash awarded by Governor Otis Bowen in 1977.

A man of the highest integrity, impeccable character, and long-range vision, Bill Barnes' long years of service and noteworthy accomplishments easily qualify him as the "dean" of conservationists, natural resource managers, and environmentalists in Indiana.

And now Bill has completed an important and interesting chronicle of the acquisition and protection of federal and state lands during the Great Depression. All citizens of Indiana are indebted to him for creating this work. Who else except

William B. Barnes, Sr. would complete such a fine volume on Indiana conservation history during his sunset years at well past 90—and while legally blind?

Friend and Colleague,

Marion T. Jackson, Professor Emeritus
Plant Ecology
Indiana State University

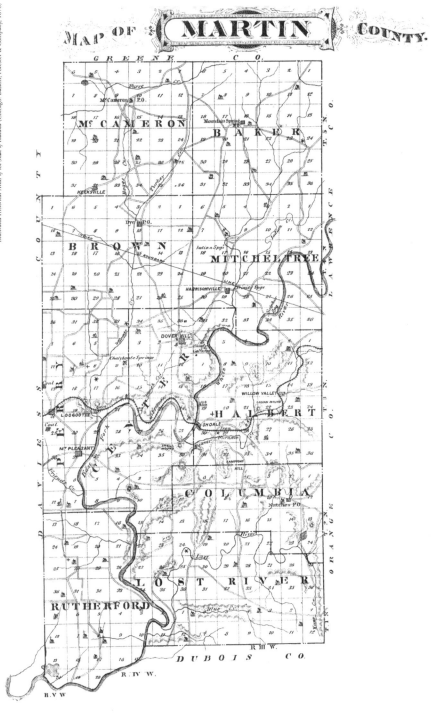

Illustrated Historical Atlas of the State of Indiana (Chicago: Baskin, Forester & Company, 1876)

A Perspective on Martin County and Its Natural Resources

The creation of this planet involved millions of years with only minor utilization of its natural wealth. The period from early exploration to the present time has been only a fleeting moment in the history of the land that is Indiana and elsewhere, but subsequent impacts on its natural resources have been great. The renewable forest and wildlife resources felt the first major effects of European settlement, but in following years, soil, water, and fish were affected as well.

Exploitative practices occurred until it became evident that the depletion of this original wealth required conservation measures. State laws were first passed for the protection of fish and wildlife. Old-growth forests were disappearing, and forest fires were further reducing poorer second-growth stands. Laws were soon passed for protection of private properties. Erosion of farmland was causing losses of valuable topsoil layers. Pollution of streams and rivers adversely affected fish, wildlife, and human health. Thus, the exploitation of natural resources was followed by the passage of conservation laws. In Indiana, the preservation of the natural environment began with the creation of the state park system in 1916 and has continued with the 1967 passage of the Nature Preserves Act. Areas were identified and dedicated for preservation.

E.T. Cox, *Second Report of the Geological Survey of Indiana Made during the Year 1870* (Indianapolis, 1871), frontispiece

Jug Rock is a well-known rock formation in Martin County.

river. Cedar Bluff, a single column standing in an open field near River Road, is the next example before passing House Rock. Within the town limits of Shoals is Jug Rock, an outstanding representative of the Mansfield Formation. Shoals High School has chosen it to represent their school. The phenomenon is located on a steep slope a short distance from U.S. highways 50 and 150. This urn-shaped column sits on a wider-based rock. During the long period when various layers of sedimentary sandstone were being deposited in the lower Pennsylvanian period, the strata evidently differed in hardness. When subsequent erosion occurred, the softer layers were less resistant to weathering. It is quite narrow at the top where it supports a large flat slab of harder rock formed at a later date.

The Pinnacle is on this high escarpment close to Jug Rock. In summer, there is a beautiful panoramic view of Shoals and the East Fork of White River bordered by fields of cropland. Both of these outstanding natural features have recently been acquired by the Indiana Department of Natural Resources, Division of Nature Preserves, but past development of homes on the upper Pinnacle has restricted its public use. A short distance above the entrance road to the Pinnacle, on the opposite side of U.S. highways 50 and 150, is Overlook

This photograph shows a 1936 winter view of the East Fork of White River from the top of the Pinnacle close to Jug Rock.

Park. It has a shelter house and picnic tables. Especially during the fall foliage season, there is a beautiful view of the East Fork of White River.

Gormerly's Bluff stands at a bend in the river about one mile downstream from Shoals. It was known by this name in the early part of the 1900s, but was later identified as Bluffs of Beaver Bend on highway maps. In 1885, Thomas Gormerly made a forty-foot-long excavation into the base of the bluff in an unsuccessful search for gold. The original main road between Shoals and Loogootee passed by the end of the escarpment. Spout Spring flows from the same rock base. Local people used to drive their horse-drawn vehicles to the spring to fill containers with the crystal-clear water. Later, motorists stopped for a refreshing drink. Past floods have inundated this valley. About fifteen feet above the spring, the date of March 28, 1913 is inscribed; this may indicate the high water mark of the 1913 flood.

This former road curved around the bluff and crossed an iron-truss bridge over the mouth of Beaver Creek where it flows into the East Fork. The scene today shows a yellow and ochre colored sandstone bluff rising vertically for a height of around eighty feet. One large rock that has broken away from the cliff rests above the riverbank. It is covered with ferns, flowering plants, and shrubs. Fifty-eight different trees and shrubs were recorded on a cursory inspection of the tract, as well as a good variety of ferns and wildflowers.

A gravel road runs along the riverbank that is well-forested with a stand of sycamore, box elder, elm, hackberry, and silver maple. Low clumps of water willow plants grow in the shallow water along the shoreline. The steep banks and side slopes between the river and the base of the bluffs have a soil mixture of silt from floodwaters and sand from the weathering sandstone rock. This combination has contributed to a lush growth of plants, aided by a cool moist exposure. American beech and sugar maple dominate some stands, with associated species of basswood, wild black cherry, black walnut, tulip poplar, white ash, and bitternut hickory. The understory layer is composed of young sugar maple and other tree species, as well as grapevine, paw paw, redbud, ironwood, spicebush, woodbine, and some poison ivy. Many areas are covered with a dense growth of wild hydrangea.

At the top of the cliff and on an adjoining ridge an entirely different habitat is encountered. The forest type changes to oak-hickory, being composed of scarlet, black, and white oaks interspersed with pignut hickory and the interesting winged elm. The thin mantle of soil on the top of the sandstone bluff supports low thickets of blueberry under some dwarf Juneberry trees. Fringes of polypody fern occur where enough soil is available in eroded rock crevices. The composition of plants on the forest floor also exhibits the difference in moisture. Lichens and mosses grow on the more exposed sites, while tangles of greenbrier and coralberry are found under ironwood, black gum, shining sumac, flowering dogwood, and young oaks. Partridge berry, lespedezas, and goldenrods are other herbs. Thus, this interesting tract offers a variety of sites from the wet riverbank to the dry xeric top. This elevation also provides a beautiful view of the river upstream toward Shoals. This outstanding beautiful and scenic natural area has been acquired by the Indiana Department of Natural Resources, Division of Nature Preserves.

Callahan's Bluff is a formation between Houghton Bridge and Hindostan Falls. It is the only location where the river covers the base of this escarpment. In future years, the water currents will continue to erode the sandstone. This outcrop can be best viewed from a boat. However, it is also accessible on the landside by a short walk from the road between Whitfield and Brooks Bridge.

Hindostan Falls, the best-known natural area in the county, is the next point of interest. The solid bottom of Mansfield sandstone extends upstream for a considerable distance. The falls is around four-feet high during low water periods. The area between the falls and Flat Rock varies in depth and contains rock fragments and detritus. Flat Rock is another example of the deposition and hardness of different layers of Mansfield sandstone. River currents continue to erode its upstream side. This once was the site of a gristmill. Evidence can be seen by a row of holes where heavy timbers supported the structure before it was destroyed by floodwaters.

Lindley Rock looms above the river at its first bend below Flat Rock. It is another high escarpment on the river. A portion of the hill above has enough soil to support hardwoods. There is a recessed area in the rock above the river. This "rock shelter" was, no doubt, used by Native Americans. There is another exposed rock area just above Brooks Bridge. The rare pinnatifid spleenwort grows on the rock at this location. The valley spreads out below this bridge. Haw Creek empties on the west side. Farther downstream Lost River, an underground stream in the Mitchell Plain in Orange County, emerges before flowing into the river in Martin County.

During the first part of the twentieth century, natural formations and their scenic beauty were taken for granted by local people, with little attention being given to their potential tourist value. With present-day interest in travel and protection of the environment, they are now considered an economic asset. It is fortunate that the county has been blessed with so many outstanding formations. They will remain that way unless blemished by man.

Recreation

In the early days, Hindostan Falls was a popular place for local and surrounding county residents. Visitors from Bedford, Orleans, Paoli, and Washington drove over gravel roads and mingled with people from Shoals and Loogootee. There were no swimming pools in the towns of Shoals and Loogootee. The water below the falls offered a refreshing place to cool off when the river was not high. Children and other poor swimmers were warned about the danger in the whirlpool between Flat Rock and the opposite bank. Some lives were lost over the years in the fast current. Tent camping became important for fishermen and families wishing to stay overnight, especially on weekends and holidays. Most campers pitched their tents under the large silver maples between the river and high bank. Other persons had small cabins on the high upstream bank above the falls.

Before swimming pools were common, bathers from Loogootee enjoyed cool water at Hindostan Falls, circa 1920.

In 1921, Chester Clements constructed a frame building with a canvas top for a dance hall. It overlooked the falls, and he operated it until 1925. A dance band from Washington, Indiana, provided the music. There was also a separate concession stand. A nearby path went down the steep bank to the edge of the water. Fishermen stood in the shallow water above and below the falls when the river was low. They also fished in the whirlpool and slack water on the downstream side of Flat Rock.

Between 1935 and 1940, I fished in the East Fork of White River at Shoals and Hindostan Falls. My fishing method differed at Shoals. I usually used either fresh or sour mussel meat placed on a hook on an attached line above a bell sinker for the fast water below the bridges. I caught mostly channel and flathead catfishes and an occasional spotted bass. When the river was low during those drought years, Alton Hawkins and I would sometimes stand on the edge of a riffle and fish in the deeper pool below it. A light tap on a small hook baited with a morsel of mussel meat resulted in the catch of redhorse sucker. His wife Lucille scored and cooked them in deep fat for eating the fine bones with the rest of the fillet.

In the late 1930s, I fished with my brother-in-law at Hindostan Falls. The dance hall was no longer there. My brother-in-law, Chet Clements, knew every hole as a result of a lifetime of fishing there. He remembered the earlier capture of a small sturgeon that tried to swim over the falls. When the river was low, we used the path on the steep bank that led to the upper rim of the falls and fished in the water below it. Channel and flathead catfishes were our favorites, but the catches varied with fresh-water drum (white perch), white bass, and an occasional sauger. Hellgrammites, minnows, and worms were the usual baits used with rods with regular spooling reels. There were very few split bamboo rods or level winding Pflugar or South Bend reels. We did not know about the early Mitchell spinning reels. Some persons cast artificial lures, and a few fly fishermen tried their luck in the water below the falls. Others fished in the whirlpool and slack water below Flat Rock. Local storms sometimes caused the river to be too high for fishing without a boat.

Otherwise, the area between Shoals and Hindostan provided many more fish than bank fishing. Persons having boats used trotlines with up to fifty hooks, and some limb lines were tied to overhanging branches along the banks. Hooks were baited with live minnows, worms, cheese and dough mixtures, and other types of bait. As long as the bait lasted, fish were continuously available. In addition to catfish, catches included buffalo, carp, white perch, and other species. A few paddlefish (spoonbills) became entangled in trotlines. An occasional person boasted about capturing a large catfish in a submerged hollow log. Illegal traps and nets were not uncommon.

NONRENEWABLE RESOURCES

Coal

The extreme eastern edge of the major coalfield in the Wabash Lowland Region extends into the western part of Martin County. Some thin seams were exposed on side hills. Where available, these deposits were used for heating in early days, and some landowners mined thicker layers for sale as late as the Great Depression. There was also one underground mine in Martin County. The use of this mineral fuel has continued where deposits are thick enough for open-cut mining.

Present-day surface mining with large earth-moving equipment has resulted in the creation of vast areas of grassland. When the topsoil is pushed back and the hard pan is compacted by heavy equipment, it has been reported that this acts as a barrier to the penetration of tree roots. The original fertile soils in nearby Daviess County are now covered by vast expanses of grassland that remind one of the short grass prairie regions of the Dakotas. Woodlots have been destroyed, squirrels are gone, and there is little escape or winter cover for all species of indigenous wildlife.

Natural Gas and Oil

A small gas field south of Loogootee provided gas for the early glass factories and for some homes there during the first twenty-five years of the 1900s. Beautiful ornate fixtures were then replaced upon the advent of electrical power. An oil well was still pumping on the John Larkin property on the south edge of Loogootee in the early 1920s. The limited gas and oil resources had been exhausted by this time, and no new fields had been discovered. Natural gas and oil are presently exhausted, and coal reserves are near depletion in Martin County. Once exhausted, they are all gone forever as nonrenewable resources.

Bedrock Deposits

The few small limestone deposits are of little significance when compared with adjoining counties in the Mitchell Plain. Conversely, exposed and underground deposits of sandstone are widespread. These deposits provided much income at Loogootee at the turn of the century. Sandstone quarried from a location near the south side of U.S. highways 50 and 150, east of the town, furnished the ground sand used in the glassworks that flourished during that period. These facilities primarily produced bottles and other similar containers. The reason for not using this particular sand for other clear glass products was probably due to its iron content. After the industry left Loogootee in 1911, the quarry was used by naked boys who dove from the high side into the deep water for recreation. This pastime continued for many years until an owner became concerned when tort lawsuits became popular. Sandstone for buildings and other purposes is in such great supply that exhaustion is highly unlikely.

Other Resources

A deposit of quartz pebbles near Spout Spring was also ground for production of refractory firebricks. These bricks were used for lining steam boilers with high temperatures. This operation existed for a short time. Ceramic clay deposits provided the source of more income. Kilns in Shoals and Loogootee produced brick and field tile. There are some older homes and other buildings constructed with bricks. Field tile, for drainage of land with tight soils, greatly aided crop production. Sand and gravel beds along the East Fork of White River are relatively limited because of its narrow valley for deposition of this material when compared with watercourses in glaciated counties. Meltwater from Illinois glaciation backed into this main river and Furse Creek in the extreme northwestern corner of the county. It dropped some sand and gravel. Small stream valleys in the hilly section contain creek gravel resulting from weathered sandstone fragments washed from higher elevations. Iron, the only metal in the area, is found in Mansfield sandstone. In early days, slabs were picked up and hauled to Ironton, near Shoals. There they were ground and refined for pig iron.

Today, the abundance and values of all of these nonrenewable resources vary. Ceramic clays are plentiful for making bricks for buildings and for drain tiles. They are first in value among this group. Quartz pebble deposits for refractory

E.T. Cox, *Second Report of the Geological Survey of Indiana Made During the Year 1870* (Indianapolis, 1871)

Around 1911, the Pines Hotel was one of the resorts at Trinity Springs, Indiana.

materials are limited for future use and value. Sand and gravel beds are not extensive, and the washed product comes from outside sources. The low content of iron in abundant Mansfield sandstone does not warrant refining. Gypsum deposits will last for years and will continue to be the most important economic material.

A New Deal in Martin County

Everyone knew that there had been a depression since the crash of the stock market in October 1929; the country's economic situation had become progressively worse by the end of 1932. No town escaped the consequences of Black Tuesday. At Loogootee, local stores and supporting businesses functioned in accordance with the needs of the community. Prices were low, and expenditures were only made for basic commodities. For example, Carnahan Manufacturing Company, managed by Fred Brooks, continued to operate, but with far fewer orders. Orders for shirts also decreased at the Reliance Company, and the Union Bank functioned only as a result of a bank merger. The once thriving pearl button factories—Gwin's in Shoals and Ward Chandler's in Loogootee—had already been adversely affected by a decrease in the sale of clothing and increased use of plastic buttons. The same conditions existed at Shoals; Donald Overton, the manager of the Hincher plant, reported a decreased demand for his product, wooden folding chairs.

Trinity Springs, formerly Harrisonville, no longer operated as a spa. When I visited it in 1936, some of the vacated two-story frame hotels still stood along the main street. Others had burned down. A deteriorated old building contained a rotting bowling ball rack and still held some bowling balls machined from heavy lignum vitae or other wood. My axe just bounced off one that I tried to split. Sulphur water bubbled up from the ground nearby.

With the New Deal a fortunate change took place in the philosophy for solving problems. In March 1933, a number of agencies were created in an effort to improve the management of natural resources. Statewide conservation measures involved soil, water, forest, fish, and wildlife. Immediate actions were taken to solve many conservation problems.

Funding for agencies started by the federal government required participation by the state of Indiana. This function was assumed by the Indiana Department of Conservation and its divisions of forestry, fish and game, and state parks, lands, and waters. The former conservation commission was abolished, and Virgil M. Simmons became the single commissioner with Kenneth M. Kunkle, assistant commissioner. Ralph F. Wilcox was director (state forester) of the Division of Forestry. Kunkle also was the director of the Division of Fish and Game, and Myron L. Reese was the director of the Division of State Parks, Lands and Waters. Later, the titles changed to the Indiana Department of Natural Resources, Division of Fish and Wildlife and Division of State Parks.

The Division of Fish and Game launched a statewide program in 1933 to increase wildlife populations. Later, some of the division's activities were found to be of only minor significance in increasing wildlife populations, but these activities were of major importance from a public relations standpoint. Statewide conservation club organizations proved to be very popular with sportsmen. By June 1935, 508 conservation clubs with an annual individual membership fee of twenty-five cents were holding regular meetings. The state was divided into sixteen districts in accordance with their populations. Each county elected a president and a district representative.

These sixteen district representatives sat on the State Conservation Committee, which met every three months. Honorary members of the Izaac Walton League, Fish, Game and Forest Organization, and state adjutant of the American Legion attended the meetings. Discussions primarily concerned fish and game along with other departmental matters. The State Conservation Committee was active in sponsoring legislation. In order to inform conservation club members, the publication *Outdoor Indiana* began in February 1934. It was mailed free of charge to club members and other interested persons. By June 30, 1935, circulation reached 80,000 monthly issues.

The most popular conservation club activities were propagating bobwhite quail and ring-necked pheasants and raising fish. The Division of Fish and Game delivered day-old ring-necked pheasant or bobwhite quail chicks that were placed in brooding pens with double runways. The birds were fed for eight weeks

Conservation Club Poster, circa 1938.

before being released on private land where farmers permitted hunting. This division paid clubs seventy-five cents for each released bird. Larger clubs constructed fish ponds and clubhouses on their properties. The division's annual budget included major expenditures for artificial propagation and raising fish.

Land Utilization Projects

In the 1930s, the U.S. Department of Agriculture, Agricultural Adjustment Administration, Land Utilization Section initiated an investigation of land use capabilities in every county in cooperation with Purdue University. In this study, each local county committee prepared a county map that showed the suggested proper land uses. Cultural practices were depicted as areas best suited for cropland, pastures, forestry, recreation, and other uses.

Martin County's committee classified land as ridge top, overflow, gently rolling, and unsuitable for agriculture. Proper uses for ridge top land included 50 percent in farming and 50 percent in woods. Farmed areas could contain 20 percent in corn, 20 percent in small grain, and 60 percent in grasses. Recommended uses of overflow land were 70 percent cropland with 50 percent in corn, 20 percent in small grains, and 30 percent in grasses. The remaining 30 percent of the overflow area included timber bordering the East Fork of White River, streams, and other wetlands. Gently rolling land was of lesser significance in the county. Forest management was recommended for large acreages classified as unsuitable for agriculture. No recommendations were made for recreational areas: this classification referred to counties with large cities and towns needing parks and open spaces. "Other use" meant land in large cities and towns; that did not apply to Martin County.

After completing investigations of land use, four counties were selected with areas best suited for public ownership. The federal government did not choose to retain full ownership; a state agency had to be found for future administration and management. The Indiana Department of Conservation agreed to sponsor these projects on a long-term lease. The Division of State Parks, Lands, and Waters chose Ripley and Pulaski counties, and the Division of Forestry chose Brown and Martin counties. The two forestry areas were acquired by the U.S. Department of Agriculture, Agricultural Adjustment Administration and designated national recreational demonstration areas. The sites included submarginal areas in Ripley County, on the north and south sides of U.S. Highway 50 east of

Versailles and in Pulaski County in north-central Indiana. The Brown County Land Utilization Tract, selected by the Division of Forestry, included a portion of rugged terrain east of Nashville and north of State Highway 46.

Federal programs that brought benefits to Indiana and Martin County included the Civilian Conservation Corps (March 1933–1941), the Agricultural Adjustment Act/Agricultural Adjustment Administration (May 1933–circa 1935), the Works Progress Administration (April 1935–1943), the Resettlement Administration (May 1935–1937), and the Farm Security Administration, which absorbed the activities of the Resettlement Administration in 1937.

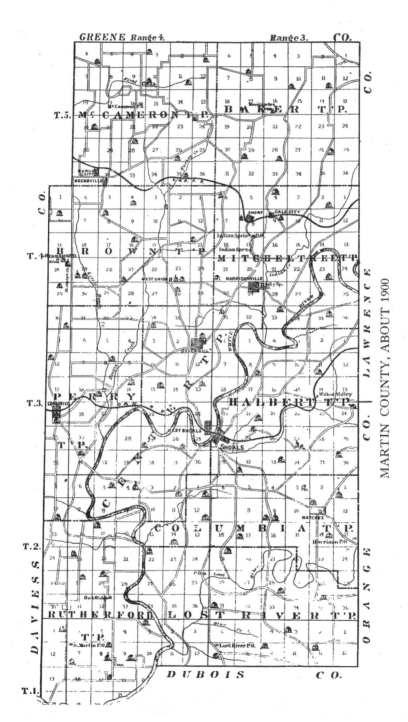

Harry Q. Holt, *History of Martin County Indiana* (Paoli, Ind. 1953), facing page 79

MARTIN COUNTY, ABOUT 1900

THE CIVILIAN CONSERVATION CORPS

By the time the Civilian Conservation Corps (CCC) program was inaugurated for the employment of young men in 1933, the Great Depression had entered its fourth year. For these young men, an army cot and good meals were a welcome change from walking the streets in search of work. These lads, between eighteen and twenty-five years of age, received $30 per month, of which $25 was sent to their families. The remaining $5 provided many amenities in those days.

Enrollees performed tasks in accordance with the mission of each camp. The Indiana Department of Conservation already had a nucleus of state properties to which it could assign enrollees in the CCC camps. The Division of Forestry initiated forest management practices along with building facilities for recreation. All of these activities stimulated local interest in the new state forests.

The Division of State Parks utilized CCC labor on its properties for historical and recreational purposes. New roads and parking lots serviced picnic areas with shelterhouses, tables, benches, fireplaces, and ovens. Hiking trails traversed sections of scenic and natural beauty. Spring Mill State Park featured the restoration of a pioneer village and had a double camp, with twice as many workers. The Division of Fish and Game also had a double camp, where a 1,400-acre marsh began to attract waterfowl. Greater sandhill cranes returned to the Jasper-Pulaski Fish and Wildlife Area and gradually increased their migrating population into thousands.

Martin County was the recipient of a CCC camp during the early period of the New Deal. Funded by the federal government, the CCC received full cooperation from the Indiana Department of Conservation. The Division of Forestry sponsored the CCC camp in Loogootee. In early June 1933, a tent camp was set up near the old ballpark in Loogootee; barracks replaced the tents in the fall. U.S. Army officers supervised the feeding, housing, and transportation of the 200 enrollees to work sites. Civilian personnel had charge of all work in the field. Camp superintendent Warren Palmer, camp forester Waldimar Hanson, a camp engineer, and a number of foremen worked with each enrollee crew. Some of these foremen were Harry Dickerson, Mr. Owens, and two Loogootee residents, John Gootee and Frank Lents.

The Division of Forestry, under State Forester Ralph F. Wilcox, had already started to acquire land northeast of Shoals for the Martin County State Forest (now Martin State Forest). Construction began on a service building, shelter house, fire tower, and roads. Timber stand improvement, erosion control, and tree planting took place on several hundred acres. Additional work was also done to control erosion on private land in other parts of the county. Check dams placed in gullies held back the soil. A nursery adjoining the camp provided black locust seedlings for planting on eroded sites.

CCC in Dubois County

While employed by the Florida Forest Service, I received a telegram from Assistant State Forester Joseph Kaylor concerning work in the CCC program in Indiana. Kaylor had been an upperclassman at the Pennsylvania State Forest School in Mont Alto that I attended (now a campus of Pennsylvania State University). On June 13, 1933, I reported at the state forester's office, which was located in a room in the basement of the State Capitol building in Indianapolis. Other young foresters and I walked to the Kahn Clothing Company on Capitol Avenue. Measurements were taken for campaign hats, green shirts, pants, and knee-high leather boots. I then drove my Model A Ford to Jasper, Indiana.

Camp 1513 was located in a woodlot leased from Mr. Gutzweiller, who had a meat processing building on another part of the tract. Our wooded area adjoined the south line of the property, which later contained Calumet Lake. The army had set up a large tent camp, with a central area with tables under a large overhead canvas cover for serving meals. Our tent, on a wooden platform, contained two beds, chairs, and a small folding table. It functioned very well during the summer months. A stove, with an outside vent pipe, later provided heat until the completion of the barracks just before Thanksgiving.

My first order of business was to report to camp superintendent Thadias Shirey. He was an older graduate at Mont Alto, too. Other civilian personnel included camp engineer Leonard Lictenberg, and foremen Jack Hill, Ralph Brunett, Robert Akester, and Warren Spalding. Paul Schneider and Michael Kress were local employees.

Initially, many changes occurred among the military personnel. Lieutenant Norman Shortridge served, and Dr. Dillon Geiger was camp physician. They were followed by Captain Louis E. Kruger, aided by Captain George W. Smith, and Lieutenant Frank J. Kendrick, medical reserve. A naval officer was also assigned for a short period. Shirey was soon assigned to the double camp in Clark County State Forest, and George R. Scott became camp superintendent. I supervised forestry and conservation fieldwork, and Leonard Lictenberg managed all construction activities. Other local persons who aided the camp were Dr. F. C. Jones and Clem Eckstein.

Many enrollees came from the area around Fort Wayne and Hartford City in northeastern Indiana. Each person received a standard issue of clothing for different seasons, a kit of army utensils, and a canteen. Each camp had another official designation in accordance with its major function. Our E.C.W. 63PE was assigned to Emergency Conservation Work involving erosion control on private land; erosion control was a priority. The Soil Conservation Service soon assumed this function. Clem Eckstein, who owned a sawmill in Jasper, greatly assisted in locating and signing up local landowners who were having erosion problems.

Establishing a nursery to raise black locust seedlings for erosion control became the first major activity. Several acres were rented on the Joseph Kempert farm north of the camp. Wilcox had recognized the need and purchased hundreds of pounds of seeds, including a full fifty-five-gallon drum at our location. Immediate work began on making raised four-foot-wide beds. After seeding, rolling, and watering, the areas were covered with straw to hasten germination. All planting operations were completed by July 4, much later than the regular seeding period in spring. We produced sufficient seedlings to also supply another camp.

Army trucks with sides, long benches, and overhead canvas covers transported groups of about twenty men to work sites. The trucks then returned to camp in order to bring hot food containers for noon meals. A foreman and squad leader, usually an older enrollee, were assigned to each truck. The army needed other enrollees to drive trucks and to serve as cooks, orderlies for tents and barracks, chauffeurs, and for other duties.

Although the Division of Forestry was responsible for supervision of conservation work, salaries for all civilian employees came from federal funds. These funds were also used to purchase and maintain motorized equipment, tools, supplies, and materials. A central supply depot and major equipment repair facility was at Morgan-Monroe State Forest, where a double camp of 400 enrollees was located. All fiscal matters were handled by a staff in the central office of this division in Indianapolis.

A contract was awarded to build living quarters for the Jasper Camp. Barracks were aligned along a company street adjoining the south side of the woodlot. Other buildings included one for recreation and separate living quarters for army and civilian personnel. The large mess hall also had a separate area for this group. Meals averaged around $15 per month. Since there was no charge for living quarters, my

Enrollees gather outside the camp kitchen at the CCC Camp at Loogootee, 1933–1934.

salary of $150 per month was quite adequate, especially when compared with the $60 paid by the Florida Forest Service.

An educational instructor was employed for the project. Classes for different subjects were voluntary. I taught dendrology to help with the identification of trees. I do not recall other subjects, but credits were not given toward a high school diploma.

Crews primarily worked on gully and sheet erosion control in the hilly terrain in eastern Dubois County where erosion was so bad in many fields that they could no longer be used for crops. Check dams were built with logs or rocks. Landowners permitted unmerchantable trees to be cut for use as logs and poles to be placed across gullies. A trench was dug in the bottom as well as another on each side of the ditch to prevent washouts. Cross logs were chinked with straw or broom sedge grass where needed, and the structure was stabilized with number nine wire. A weir notch, cut in the top log, permitted water to flow through and empty on a pole spillway below. The back part of the dam was filled with soil. The areas above gullies had also lost topsoil due to sheet erosion. In order to retard runoff, brush was placed between two parallel lines of stakes driven into the subsoil. Erosion control continued on private land during the winter of 1933–1934.

These barracks replaced tents at the CCC Camp at Loogootee.

In the spring of 1934, black locust seedlings were planted on all properties where erosion control work had been completed. Some Virginia pines were added to determine if this conifer would eventually invade black locust. A forester from the central office visited our camp to teach the proper way to plant a tree. He used the two-man method, having one enrollee use a grub hoe for digging the hole and the other insert the plant before compacting it. This method was slow on open areas, but was necessary where each hole had to be first scalped of competing vegetation. When I worked at the Florida Forest Service, we used a planting bar; I later replaced the grub hoe with this implement on open areas.

While the Jasper Camp was in operation, some work crews were assigned to the area east of Ferdinand. Remedial measures in conservation of soil resources attracted the attention of farmers in that vicinity during the summer of 1933. Henry Tretter soon led a drive among his neighboring landowners to give land for a new state forest. Other interested persons gave money, and the Indiana Division of Forestry received a gift of 868 acres.

It was necessary to clear land titles, but some tracts became available in the winter of 1933–1934. This made it possible to make preliminary plans for various kinds

Hot lunches were delivered to each CCC work site in metal containers like those in the foreground.

of work. Erosion control continued, and thousands of black locust seedlings were planted on state and local land. A property owned by Frank Seng was purchased for location of a fire tower at a high elevation. Materials, supplies, and equipment had to be requisitioned for planned buildings, roads, and a dam for a new lake.

Many of these activities took place while the camp was still at Jasper and entailed long drives from Jasper to the new Ferdinand State Forest. The barracks at Jasper, completed by Thanksgiving, now had to be moved to the north side of Ferdinand. As building construction had been by sections, it was much easier to dismantle and move them for occupancy by May 1934. When the camp became a state property, the emergency conservation designation changed to S576.

We planted black locust and conifers after the frost was out of the ground, in accordance with our spring plans. However, 100,000 conifers that had not been ordered were delivered during the first week in May. When the Division of Forestry had not sold all of its stock, the surplus had to be planted on state property. The two-year-old Norway spruce and the white, red, Virginia, and Scotch pine conifers had all started to grow with elongated new shoots. They were all planted within a short time frame. While 90 percent survival is normal, advanced growth

Staff at Dubois County CCC included: George R. Scott, camp superintendent; a naval officer; Leonard Lictenberg, camp engineer; Warren Spalding, foreman; and unknown individual.

and hot, dry periods caused a poor survival rate despite hoeing around the plants in midsummer.

Hurricane Creek provided the site for a forty-two-acre lake with fish-rearing ponds. Constructing this lake and building roads were major projects during the summer and early fall. Trees were hand dug from the future lake and cut flush with the ground five feet from the future shoreline. Fortunately, most of this area was already cleared. Construction at the dam began as soon as title was cleared on the property. A cutoff trench was excavated below the ground level. A heavy rain retarded progress when it filled the deep trench, and a pump had to be installed to remove the water. Upon completion of a large, square, concrete culvert with a vertical section extending to the desired water level of the lake, earth-filling operations began and a water line to the fish-rearing ponds was constructed. The fill material for this dam was hand dug by six enrollees assigned to each dump truck. At some borrow pits, it was necessary to loosen the soil with dynamite. This and other projects were designed to provide work.

Purdue University, in cooperation with the Division of Forestry, also initiated a study about the forest resources of Dubois County. Landowners with woods on their

Enrollees at this CCC camp in Jasper, Indiana, worked on erosion control in 1933, and in 1934, on Ferdinand State Forest projects at the Ferdinand CCC Camp.

properties gave permission to inventory timber resources. I selected and trained enrollees to make 10 percent timber cruises of each wooded area. These three-man parties measured and tallied by species all trees six inches or higher D.B.H. (diameter breast height). A one-chain-wide strip (sixty-six feet) was used in every tenth strip. These data were then submitted for calculations of timber volumes.

During 1934, a fire tower was erected, and work began on structures near the dam. Camp engineer Leonard Lictenberg, with the assistance of new foremen Herbert Murnan and Robert MacKlin, supervised all construction. Local WPA (Works Progress Administration) crews included some skilled persons for more detailed construction assignments. Samuel Saperie, chief engineer for the Indiana Department of Conservation, made inspection trips. I stayed with this project until I was transferred to Bluffton in northern Indiana in February 1935. My new assignment concerned the new Wells County State Forest and Game Preserve (now Ouabache State Park).

This CCC crew built this high check dam across a deep gully caused by erosion.

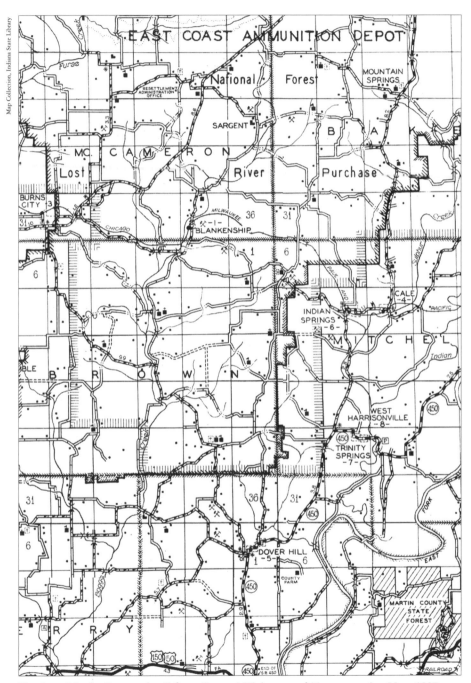

Northern Martin County, detail from General Highway and Transportation Map, 1937, state roads revised to January 1949.

SOUTHERN INDIANA AGRICULTURAL DEMONSTRATION PROJECT

The Southern Indiana Agricultural Demonstration Project in Martin County was designated by the U.S. Department of Agriculture to consist of 32,000 acres. However, the Martin County State Forest had been started as a separate forest area at an earlier date. The project area over time had several different designations. Selection of the three northern townships was well justified. Submarginal land use, primarily due to physical features, had greatly affected the economy of the area and had exerted a great influence on its human population, roads, and schools.

A population decline in these three townships indicated a decrease in farming prosperity. McCameron Township dates to 1828. Between 1900 and 1940, Frank Garrett operated the Burns City Nursery Company, which was the only important off-farm employer in the township and used some sixty people during peak seasonal operations. Sawmills also employed locals as did the Milwaukee, St. Paul and Pacific Railroad. By 1930, only 607 persons resided in McCameron Township.

In 1837, Baker Township was established in the northwest corner of the county. Mountain Springs was platted in 1849 and had a post office by 1850. However, it remained a small community with a store, church, and few houses; it lost its post office in 1905. By 1930, the population of Baker Township was merely 483. Brown Township was not created until 1841. There was no platted town, but the small community of Bramble, with a church, store, and several homes located on the western side of the township, had 643 people in 1930. The north lines of McCameron and Baker townships coincided with the Martin-Greene County line; the east side of Baker Township bordered Lawrence County. Mitcheltree Township bordered the south line of Baker and east line of Brown, while Perry Township met Brown Township's south line. A few tracts in Perry and Mitcheltree townships were optioned.

The western edge of the project area roughly followed a line between the high hills of the unglaciated upland and the rolling terrain of the glaciated Wabash Lowland. In McCameron Township, it extended from a point east of the present town of Crane, southward to the hills east of Burns City and the area just east of Bramble in Brown Township.

In this area, later called the Southern Indiana Land Utilization Demonstration Project, physiographic features were similar to those of many other parts of the county. Valleys were narrower due to their locations on upper watersheds. There was some exposed sandstone bedrock at the Rock House in McCameron Township, as well as other outcrops and overhangs elsewhere. Several springs of varying sizes marked the cleavage points between different rock strata. Mountain Springs in Baker Township had the largest water discharge. A few small caves also existed between limited limestone outcrops and upper sandstone strata.

Watersheds in the Project Area

There were two drainage systems in the project area. The smaller one emptied into the West Fork of White River. The stream that drained this northwest corner had been called variously, First, Furst, Furse, and Furs Creek. These names may have been derived from the word "Furs." However, the name Furse, which was shown on an early map in 1876, will be used in this text.

High ridges in the northern portion of McCameron Township bounded the drainage area of Furse Creek. The northern edge of the watershed line meandered slightly into Greene County. However, much of the project area contained streams in the watershed of the East Fork of White River. Boggs Creek drained the southwestern part of McCameron Township and continued to flow into the northern part of Brown Township to its confluence with Turkey Creek. Turkey Creek started in the northwest corner of Baker Township and flowed southwesterly through eastern McCameron Township to the above-described confluence. Drainage in Baker Township primarily involved Sulphur Creek, which began near the Greene County line and flowed southeast of Mountain Springs. In a meandering course to its confluence with Little Sulphur Creek, Sulphur Creek drained an area on the west above Indian Springs.

Soils in Project Area

The soil resources of Martin County varied in accordance with topography and inherent fertility. Farms on bottomlands and moderately sloping areas were productive. Those on the hilly portions in all parts of the county had been subjected to poor land use practices. Thousands of acres, unsuitable for agriculture, had been cleared for farming. These were unproductive, and some were reverting back to forest cover. Depletion of soil fertility continued on the acres that remained in agriculture.

Soil quality and topography exert a profound influence on land use. Thin soils and steepness of slopes mandate different land use practices, especially in hill country. If present knowledge about soil management had been available in earlier times, contour strips, sodded waterways, and proper crop rotations may have helped manage these hilly areas. Soils in this area were mainly derived from weathered material including sandstones, siltstones, and shales. Ridge top soils contained loess, a wind-blown deposit from the Wabash Lowland. Soils were deep to moderately deep. Slopes varied from gentle to very steeply sloping and were well drained on ridge tops and side hills above narrow alluvial valleys. A preliminary soil survey of Martin County aided in determining inherent productivity of purchased tracts.

A series of soil consists of similar soil horizons or layers. Soils on the project area can be roughly divided into two types: uplands bordered by side hills and slopes with bottomlands below them. No effort will be made to describe all of the various soils. However, Zanesville and Wellston soils on the uplands and Wellston-Gilpin and Wellston-Berks-Gilpin Complexes on side hills and slopes, along with other minor complexes, are of major significance. Bottomland soils formed by alluvium begin in upper narrow valleys and widen downstream. These are Burnside loam and Haymond, Wakeland, and Birds silt loams. Haymond silt loam is the major type along Furse and Sulphur creeks. Burnside loam is most frequent in the upper reaches of Boggs, Turkey, and Little Sulphur creeks.

Zanesville silt loam, which occupies land on ridge tops, is a deep, moderately drained to well-drained soil capped by loess. For thousands of years, strong westerly winds blew across the Wabash Lowland, depositing coarse, heavy, sandy material in parts of Daviess and Knox counties near river courses. Some of the finer, silty material that fell on Martin County helped to create this acid silt loam. This loam varies from five to eleven inches in thickness in the surface layer, which is strongly acid. However, this layer may vary from zero to two inches on eroded sites. On slopes from 6 to 12 percent, erosion becomes a greater factor. There is a fragipan, or a hard layer of soil, in the subsurface. When dry, a fragipan tends to retard drainage.

Wellston silt loam is also found on ridge tops where slopes vary from 2 to 6 percent. Drainage is similar to Zanesville, but there is no fragipan. The typical surface layer is about ten inches thick, again varying in thickness due to erosion. This layer was also formed by loess and weathered sandstone. The subsoil is about twenty-

By the 1930s, erosion posed serious problems for farmers in Martin County. Photograph taken in May 1938.

three inches thick, and bedrock is at an approximate depth of forty-one inches. This soil is eroded on 6 to 12 percent slopes and severely eroded on slopes ranging from 12 to 18 percent.

Wellston-Gilpin Complex is found on hillsides with 12 to 30 percent slopes. In a typical profile, the surface layer of Wellston silt loam is only two inches thick, adjoining a subsurface layer of about four inches with a subsoil about forty-three inches in depth. Gilpin soil, in this same complex, has a surface layer of Channery silt loam about six inches thick. The subsoil is about twenty-seven inches in depth. Wellston-Berks-Gilpin Complex includes well-drained soils on 18 to 70 percent slopes. The combined thickness of surface and subsurface layers of the Wellston soil types is only three inches; Berks is two inches, and Gilpin four inches. Some eroded sites have no topsoil. Their subsoil layers are around twenty-six inches.

Burnside loam is the bottomland alluvial soil generally found in narrow valleys below adjoining side hills. It is occasionally flooded for brief periods. The nearly level, well-drained soil has a surface layer of five inches and subsurface of four inches. The subsoil is about twenty inches and overlies very gravelly loam above bedrock at about forty-two inches.

Ralph F. Wilcox, Indiana state forester (on left), was inspecting a deep gully in Martin County caused by erosion.

Haymond silt loam is a nearly level alluvial soil located in wide valleys. It is frequently flooded for longer periods than Burnside. The coarse, silty, nonacid soil has a surface layer of nine inches, and a fifty-inch subsoil. Underlying material extends to a depth of seventy inches.

Wakeland silt loam is coarse, silty, nonacid, and nearly level. It is somewhat poorly drained and contains a surface layer about seven inches thick. Underlying material extends to a depth of sixty inches. This alluvial soil is frequently flooded for brief periods. As valleys widen, Birds silt loam, a nearly level, deep, poorly drained soil, is also frequently flooded for long periods and is subject to ponding. The water table is often near or above the surface layer of six inches.

Soil Usages

With the exception of a few isolated woodlots, ridge tops, and side slopes, silt loams had been cleared of trees by the 1930s. Open areas were used for crops, pastures, hay fields, and occasional small apple orchards. Because of these narrow strips above steeper slopes, very few fields contained more than ten acres.

On the Wellston-Gilpin soil types, where land slopes varied from 12 to 30 percent, clearing had occurred on many tracts. Where crops were planted, the resultant loss of topsoil caused serious erosion. Many cleared fields had reverted to pastures and hay fields where the lack of proper cultural practices often caused invasion of broom sedge grass. Other fields had been abandoned and were reverting into idle land with natural succession of woody vegetation. However, a higher percentage of this land had remained in timber.

Soils in the Wellston-Berks-Gilpin Complex, on slopes that varied from 18 to 70 percent, had also experienced some land clearing. Likewise, these fields suffered a loss of soil and fertility. However, the steep slope of most sites caused them to remain in forest cover. At lower elevations, wooded ravines contained soil particles that had washed from adjoining steep side slopes. These widened into V-shaped valleys with Burnside loam. Clearing often took place where the valleys became wide enough for pastures and hay fields or a few rows of corn.

While much of the area containing both Burnside loam and Haymond silt loam had been cleared, some remained in timber. In the valleys above the confluence of Boggs and Turkey creeks in McCameron and Baker townships was Burnside loam that graded into Haymond downstream; Furse Creek and Sulphur Creek both contained Haymond silt loam. More of these alluvial soils were in cropland.

In Brown Township, where Boggs Creek became the major drainage system, the coarse, silty, non-acid Wakeland soil became dominant. It often adjoined the fine, silty, non-acid Birds soil. With the exception of Burnside loam, all of these bottomland soils were frequently flooded. Wakeland soil was poorly drained, and Birds soil was often flooded in early spring. Where proper drainage measures had not been taken, flooding caused major farming problems. Because ditching and use of tile were expensive, they were not utilized much in the upper valleys.

The boundary of the project purchase extended to southern Brown Township where the land was more intensively farmed. It should be understood that the primary objective in acquiring land for a state forest dictated the purchase of tracts unsuited for agriculture. However, an area of this size had bottomland of higher value interspersed between hilly terrain. Each tract was appraised in order to give the owner the choice to sell. This policy, however, became a problem in Furse Creek, where the Martin County Land Use Committee classified bottomland as overflow land. Its definition evidently included areas that were subject to floodwater from the East Fork of White River, as well as those occasionally or frequently flooded along stream courses in the project area. Farming took place, as described, in the valleys of Furse, Sulphur, Little Sulphur, Boggs, and Turkey creeks, but their widths were restricted within the purchase area.

Otherwise, the county committee only recommended farming on ridge tops and uplands, primarily represented by Zanesville and Wellston silt loams. These two soils were also more subject to erosion on slopes exceeding 6 percent. Since the Wellston-Gilpin and Wellston-Berks-Gilpin complexes varied in steepness from 12 to 70 percent, most had been classified as unsuitable for agriculture.

Farming Practices

Geology, soils, and other natural features influenced land use practices. Settlers and those who followed adjusted their farming practices in accordance with their desire to make a living. Unfortunately, many of the cleared fields soon lost their fertility on farms in the hill country of south-central Indiana. Farming practices in the project area differed from the corn-soybean rotation of today.

The recommended rotation was corn-small grain-legumes on cropland. Corn stalks were cut by hand and placed in shocks to permit drying. When wheat followed, it was drilled around the shocks in the early fall. After the corn had been shucked ahead of the invasion of field mice, the shocks were removed for use as fodder and bedding. Green sprouting wheat fields were evidence of the locations of the former rows of corn shocks. More progressive farmers followed this rotation, followed by legumes. In other cases, corn followed corn, or oats were seeded the following spring. This practice left bare fields subject to winter erosion. The use of legumes was a method for nitrogen replenishment—as was green manure. Farmers usually spread animal manure on fields rather than buying expensive fertilizers. Overuse of corn and obvious lack of contour farming resulted in loss of soil fertility and topsoil; fields then reverted to hay fields and pastures for livestock.

Forest Types

Hardwood forests in this part of the Midwest have long been recognized as being of the highest quality in the world. However, tree growth fluctuates with the fertility of the soil and other environmental factors. The project area with its ridges and slopes, contained some bottomlands where growth was faster.

In this hill country, the types of original forest cover were influenced by exposure, steepness of slope, and inherent soil quality. When the original survey of Indiana and Martin County was made and shown on General Land Office maps, one member of the survey party noted the quality of land in each section. Some contained low quality timber, but there were many magnificent stands of original hardwoods in climax types in the area.

Martin County does not now have an example of an old-growth forest. In fact, there are few left in the state. "Ancient," "virgin," or the preferable term, "old-growth," forest is used to describe the climax condition of original forest stands. Few changes took place in biodiversity. These environments, where plants and animals lived in harmony for thousands of years, existed prior to European settlement in all of the area that is now Indiana. Donaldson's Woods in Spring Mill State Park represents a pre-settlement ecosystem on rolling limestone soils. The karst topography with underground drainage supports a stand of magnificent hardwoods of white, red, and black oaks, mixed with sugar maple, beech, hickories, tulip poplar, and other species.

Pioneer Mothers Memorial Forest in the Hoosier National Forest represents a different ecosystem. Steep side slopes extend to a ridge top and support a mixture of beech, maple, oaks, and black walnut. Upper slopes and ridge tops contain more oaks and hickories and fewer sugar maple and beech. One white oak on the lower tract was estimated to be between 500 and 600 years old before it died.

U.S. Forest Service, Hoosier National Forest

The Pioneer Mothers Memorial Forest represents an ecosystem with ancient oak trees, including the dead white oak shown here.

Stands of trees in the project area were influenced by many original environmental factors. Each soil type differed in texture, inherent fertility, and capacity to hold water. Exposure direction and degree of slope were other factors. These, in turn, influenced the amount of biomass in each ecosystem. For example, the total biomass of plants and animals in an oak-hickory forest on a dry southern exposure was much less than in a mesophytic site. The same forest types still remained there with altered compositions. The oak-hickory type forest occupied ridges and upper side slopes, while the western mixed mesophytic forest type assumed dominance on some lower slopes with better moisture conditions and exposures. The beech-maple type was also found on other similar cool sites. Bottomlands had the oak, sycamore, silver maple, river birch type and other combinations. Scattered woodlots of the oak-hickory type remained on ridges and upper slopes; sites with better moisture contained white and black oaks associated with pignut and mockernut hickories.

Heavy grazing by cattle and hogs resulted in an understory quite bare of young trees, shrubs, and wildflowers. The few tracts that were not grazed, as well as those on slopes with moist cooler exposures, had good ground cover. Understory trees and shrubs were flowering dogwood, sassafras, paw paw, and other shade tolerant species. Wildflowers were not as showy as those in some other forest types. Harbinger of spring (salt and pepper) was an early bloomer along with red trillium and violets that soon mingled with mayapple and bedstraws. Christmas fern, which remained evergreen in winter, further enhanced the ground cover. Some slopes also had clumps of cigar-shaped squawroot associated with oaks. As saprophytes, they did not produce green chlorophyll and were dependent on a host plant as well as on a fungus.

On some upper dry sites, the ground was often covered with dense stands of blueberry, huckleberry, and tangles of greenbriers. There was a less showy display of wildflowers in open spaces with bluets, phlox, false Solomon's seal, and bedstraws. The driest ridges and some south facing slopes on exposed rocky and Channery soils sustained the poorest growth on these very dry places. Post oak, scarlet oak, pignut hickory, and winged elm were all slow growing species. On many spots, the ground only supported lower plant life composed of lichens (such as reindeer moss, white-bottomed cetraria, and large tube, red top, and brown top cladonias), pussytoes, spleenworts, poverty grass, and tick clover.

The beech-maple forest type, of secondary significance in the project area, occurred at lower elevations with cooler and moister conditions. Beech and both sugar and black maple were the dominant species. Associates included white oak, red oak, white ash, tulip poplar, and red elm. Understory trees and shrubs were the two hard maples, beech, red elm, flowering dogwood, red mulberry, sassafras, ironwood, and redbud. Woodbine and grape were common vines growing on trees, as well as poison ivy climbing on trees and spreading on the ground.

The more common ferns were Christmas, fragile, marginal shield, and silvery spleenwort. Woodland wildflowers varied in flowering from spring to fall. Early bloomers were spring beauty, trout lily, Dutchman's breeches, red trillium, and mayapple. In summer, the flora was further represented by various species of waterleaf, violets, bedstraws, white baneberry, Solomon's seal, and wood sorrel. Little clumps of beech drops were also interesting in that they showed the same affinity to beech trees as squawroot did to oaks.

Western mesophytic forest type, which occurred on moist lower slopes and narrow valleys, included a mixture of oaks, hickories, beech, and maples. However, the oaks were numerous, with white oak leading followed by red oak and chinquapin oak on moister sites and black oak on drier ones. Shagbark and bitternut hickories grew along with beech and hard maples. Associates were tulip poplar, black walnut, basswood, white ash, green ash, hackberry, black cherry, black gum, and other species.

Understory trees were similar to those in the beech-maple type. The more shade tolerant sugar maple and beech grew with sassafras, white and green ashes, and blue beech, but there were very few young oaks of any species. With the exception of sugar maple and beech, many of the above associates died when they reached sapling sizes. Sugar maple and beech continued to withstand the shade and grew slowly. However, when a tree died or windstorms created openings for more sunlight, the seeds of tulip poplar, ash, black cherry, black walnut, hickories, and oaks were blown in by winds or deposited by animals. These species, less tolerant of shade, reproduced and outgrew existing beech and sugar maple. Wild grape and Virginia creeper (woodbine) climbed in many trees. Mapleleaf viburnum, spicebush, paw paw, flowering dogwood, and wild hydrangea stood above ground vegetation of wild ginger, bloodroot, wild geranium, and Solomon's seal. Many different ferns included maidenhair, sensitive, broad beech, and marginal shield, along with silvery and narrowleaf spleenworts.

Bottomlands also supported mixed hardwood forest types. Trees found in upper valleys that occasionally flooded were quite similar to the mixed mesophytic. Tulip poplar, red oak, American and red elms, black walnut, and green ash became more frequent. Understory trees and shrubs were similar to those in the mesophytic type but with more blue beech and the addition of bladdernut and wahoo in the shrub layer. The herbaceous layer varied from spring to fall with the same appearance of wild ginger, trilliums, wild geranium, and Jack-in-the-pulpit, followed in mid-summer by less showy knotweed, sweet cicily, poison ivy, Solomon's seal, violets, bedstraws, sensitive fern, silvery spleenwort, tall bellflower, and large blue lobelia.

The wetter bottomland downstream caused some changes to take place in plant life. This was quite evident in Brown Township and south of the project area, where the valley of Boggs Creek widened and was frequently flooded. Silver maple, sycamore, cottonwood, river birch, big shellbark hickory, swamp white oak, pin oak, Shumard's red oak, honey locust, and green ash were dominant in stands. Dominant understory trees were green ash, silver maple, boxelder, hackberry, elms, and blue beech. Shrubs included spicebush, paw paw, and redbud. The herbaceous layer consisted of jewelweed, stinging nettle, poison ivy, sedges, and cleavers bedstraw.

Forest Succession

Where cropland, pastures, and hay fields were not maintained, fields reverted to idle land. These abandoned fields were in different stages of succession back to woody cover in accordance with the number of idle years. The first invaders in cropland were ragweed, smartweed, foxtail, and other annuals, followed by asters, goldenrods, sunflowers, and other hardy perennial forbs. Broom sedge grass was a prime invader of pastures.

The symbiotic relationship between plants and animals became quite evident in the successional phases. Seeds of various species of blackberries and other plants that passed through the alimentary tracts of feeding birds created standing clumps of blackberries while dewberries and other vining vegetation spread over the ground. The next successional phase followed with the appearance of trees, shrubs, and vines. Bobwhite quail and other birds, such as robins and blue jays, likewise passed the scarified seeds of flowering dogwood, sumac, sassafras, wild grape, bittersweet, and poison ivy. Many fox scats in the fall contained persimmon seeds. Squirrels aided by burying acorns and black walnuts next to woodland edges. Windblown seeds of tulip poplar, ashes, maples, and elms produced seedlings far out in these fields as examples of natural reforestation.

This idle field is being invaded by broom sedge grass, several forbs, and tree seedlings.

Project Area Economy

The early economy of Martin County primarily relied upon income derived from the land. Early settlers had produced food for their own use and bartered or sold the surplus. They harvested timber for their own buildings or for sale. Monetary return to farmers and residents of Shoals and Loogootee fluctuated with the prosperity in the nation and state. By the time of the Great Depression economic conditions were especially harsh for people living on submarginal land where it had been difficult to make a living even in good times. Residents who owned larger tracts and better cropland were self-sufficient. Many other, less-fortunate families faced a different situation; no more than $200 in cash passed through the hands of some families during an entire year. Some younger persons, who had migrated to cities, returned home to live with their parents. Other couples found small cabins or shacks with dirt floors. There they could raise a garden or get a hog or cow to sustain their existence.

Subsistence in the country was easier than the poverty of cities. Farmers received low prices for their products; pork prices, for instance, were so low that the U.S. Department of Agriculture advocated slaughtering pigs to eliminate

This family of six was living in this log cabin in Martin County.

During the Great Depression, two couples shared this dwelling in Martin County.

overproduction. Still, food was available on farms in the form of livestock, poultry, milk, and eggs. Vegetables were grown for summer use and canned for other seasons. Surplus was sold or bartered for necessities. Farm homes and other buildings furnished shelter, especially welcomed when free from mortgages. Wells lined with native sandstone and springs provided water along with cisterns that collected runoff from buildings. Obviously, the standard of living was not high, but residents could find happiness in attending churches, reunions, and local social activities.

Thin topsoils on ridges and slopes in Martin County and some other counties, especially in the Crawford and Norman uplands regions of unglaciated south-central Indiana, had lost much of their original fertilities, and valuable tree species had been cut to augment income. Large piles of railroad ties along sidings meant that smaller trees were being harvested before they reached sizes that brought a higher price as merchantable timber. The stock was further depleted when livestock was permitted to graze in these woodlands. This practice greatly retarded reproduction of desirable young trees, caused rapid runoff resulting in erosion, and reduced moisture for trees in the overstory, while it provided only limited grazing for livestock. Woodlands suffered when the average family did not own enough land to allow any of it to remain unused, or did not have other supplementary income. It was difficult for many to continue their land ownership. Further, taxes paid by residents were insufficient to construct and maintain roads or to support schools.

Martin County Road Network

Martin County's network of roads in the project area in the 1930s was similar to that of the 1870s. Some main roads are of interest. One road began near Dover Hill and passed through West Union. It continued in a general northwesterly direction to the Old Field School and Baptist Church and ended at Burns City. Another climbed a steep hill west of Indian Springs and connected with the Dover Hill–Burns City road. In the north sector of the project, a road beginning at Mountain Springs wound in a westerly course past Sargent's Store and uphill to the future Resettlement Administration farmstead office. From here, it continued west past Salem Church, passed a country store at Buttermilk Junction, and continued to a bridge over Furse Creek before turning north to Culpepper School (now Crane). The road crossed the creek downstream below the present dam.

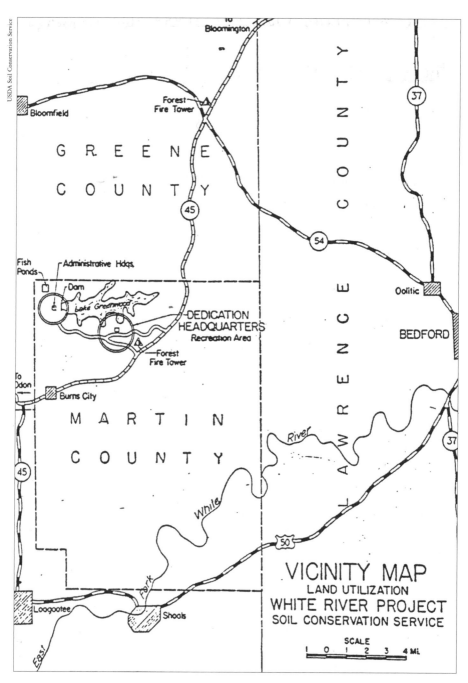

This 1939 map shows state highways in the vicinity of the project area. Highways 45 and 58 were rerouted after title to the area was transferred to the U.S. Navy in 1940.

North-south roads also serviced the area. One on the eastern edge of Baker Township led to Mt. Olive. Another connected Mountain Springs with Owensburg to the north. It also extended south to Cale, and thence west to Indian Springs. A road ran south from Sargent's Store along Turkey Creek to Blankenship and continued south into Brown Township to the project area boundary line. Other roads ran north and south from Burns City. The old Bloomfield Road could still be followed from this county seat in Greene County south to Scotland and Burns City, thence south to Loogootee.

In 1934, no state highways traversed the area, but that soon changed. In 1936, a short extension of State Highway 43 extended south from Owensburg to Mountain Springs. In 1937, the Indiana State Highway Commission started construction of State Highway 45 from Burns City to the present site of the Bloomington gate at Crane. An extension of State Highway 58 from an intersection with State Highway 45 easterly towards Bedford was proposed. It was later abandoned in the project area as was the earlier extension of State Highway 43 south of Owensburg. During the entire development period, State Highway 45 was listed as unimproved but covered with crushed stone. Roy Harp, a local resident, was the first person appointed to maintain the portion of this highway through the project area.

When the project, then called the White River Land Utilization Project, was dedicated on September 15, 1939, the U.S. Soil Conservation Service prepared a map that showed federal and state highways in that part of Martin County and adjoining areas in Greene and Lawrence counties. All roads were "unimproved" in that they were not covered by blacktop. The road from the stone quarry to the dam had crushed stone after construction. Another road from State Highway 45 to the public use area and boat facility was blacktopped at the end of the project.

Automotive traffic during inclement weather became a problem. All other roads were mostly dirt or contained some crushed limestone or creek gravel in bad spots. Chains for placement around rear tires were carried in car trunks for use during snow or wet weather. I found it became necessary to replace some tires on my coupe after 10,000 miles of travel.

Martin County Schools

Education was affected by location and condition of roads. At one time, Martin County was reported to have more one-room schools than any other county in the state. Mary Fegan Hagerty taught in many rural schools on the west side of the county for forty-seven years. One of her one-room schools near Brown Township will serve as an example of schools in the project area.

At its location on State Highway 45, north of Loogootee, children walked to the Wood School. It served approximately twenty pupils each year. It was necessary to dismiss pupils if a heavy rain caused Smith's Creek to rise in the afternoon. There was no water pump, so older boys carried buckets of water from a nearby residence and poured the water into a container for the children. Windows on two sides of the building provided the only light. This school had single seats on both sides of a coal stove with the teacher's recitation desk in front. One older boy was paid ten cents a day to come early in order to bring in coal and fire up the coal stove, as well as sweep the floor. Two outhouses provided the necessary sanitary facilities, other than the day after Halloween when they had to be placed back on their foundations.

Burns City, a village of approximately 150 inhabitants, had a small high school that also serviced the surrounding community. However, walking some distance to school was the rule. When this distance became too great, other means became

Children, who lived too far away to walk to school, took school hacks such as this one in Brown Township.

necessary. Horses or mules drew homemade hacks. These rectangular boxes on wagons had entrance doors at the rear.

At the project dedication ceremony in 1939, project manager James W. Pendry reported some interesting information about the expenses involved in providing education and transportation on this submarginal farmland. Taxes collected from landowners paid for only 10 to 15 percent of the costs for roads, schools, and other administrative charges. At that time, ten schools had already been closed, and it was estimated that one hundred miles of rural roads would be closed eventually, with the remaining sections to be maintained by the Indiana Department of Conservation, Division of Forestry.

Land Acquisition

In 1934, the U.S. Department of Agriculture, Agricultural Adjustment Administration's Land Utilization Section began to acquire farms from willing sellers. E. A. Norton was acting director in the regional office located in Urbana, Illinois. In Indiana, J. B. "Heavy" Kohlmeyer was state project director. Russell J. Otten determined the value for each tract. He had an office in Shoals near the courthouse. Lois Earl became his secretary in May 1934. Their files contained two important records. One showed a map of the purchase area. Each tract listed the owner's name, acreage, and location by section number in McCameron, Baker, and Brown townships. A few tracts were also shown in the northwest corner of Perry Township. The other record contained information on the status of each land option taken during the period September 19, 1934, through November 9, 1936.

A description of the procedure to purchase each tract was given in detail. Harrison Pruett signed the first option. It was listed as Tract B-14-8 (Tract 8 in Section 14, Brown Township): number of acres 40; total appraisal price $203.40; total option price $200.00; date of option September 19, 1934; expiration date of option March 19, 1935; and date of purchase December 20, 1935. It should be noted that Mr. Pruett's payment required fifteen months on a six-month option. This large record sheet also had another column titled "date of lease agreement." His record and many others did not show lease agreements, so I assumed that many landowners just waited for their checks without any lease renewals. Others signed this document. It covered far more than six months as attested by the difference between the date of the lease and final payment.

Before a check could be issued from Washington, D.C., the procedure required a search of the abstract in the project office and submission, recommendation, and acceptance by the regional office for each option. Very few options were closed in six months. Farms were optioned until November 9, 1936. However, only 77 of 288 options had been paid by the end of this period. The few options taken in Perry Township were later canceled.

It should be noted that the policy did not require the land buyer to reveal the appraised value to the owner. Mr. Pruett received $5.00 per acre, or $200.00 for his 40 acres that had been appraised for $203.40.

Some landowners were paid the exact appraisal to the cent, but rounding caused others to lose money. Owners of more expensive tracts might receive as much as $200 less than appraisal due to this rounding factor. Few received more than the appraised values. In a few cases, the appraised and optioned amounts were identical. Probably the so-called appraisal was the same as the assessed amount for taxation purposes in most cases. One interesting exception concerned the James W. Waggoner farm. This was the last one with some land in the future Lake Greenwood bottom. The 100-acre

NAME OF OWNER	Tract No.	No. of Acres	Option No.	Total Appraisal Price	Total Option Price	Date of Option	Expiration Date of Option	Date Optic Renew
Ackerman, Isom J.	P-33-1	20	256	140.00	130.00	7-23-35	1-23-36	
Adkins, Jane	Mc-21-13	31	213	175.75	175.00	2-23-35	8-23-35	
Allen, John T.	Mc-10-8	130	225	2002.15	2000.00	10-2-35	4-2-36	
Allen, David A.	BA-2-6	30	221	155.60	155.00	4-13-35	10-13-35	
Allen, James N.	Mc-28-1	40	254	250.10	250.00	5-21-35	11-21-35	
Amis, Oliv. J.	B-11-1							
Amis, Oliv. J.	B-12-1a	118	1	566.80	566.40	11-15-34	5-15-35	
Armstrong, Herschel	B-19-9a	B-19-9a	189	323	1973.80	3000.00	8-7-35	2-7-36	
Andis, Ira.	B-16-1	19	2	152.25	152.00	11-14-34	5-14-35	
Armstrong, John L.	B-24-1	70	194	656.13	656.00	6-5-35	12-5-35	
Arnold, John O.	Ba-11-1a	Ba-2-2	480	217	5059.28	4800.00	3-20-35	9-20-35	
Atha, Thomas & Sarah	Mc-34-2a	Mc-27-4	147	115	751.50	714.00	1-16-35	7-16-35	
Anthis, Homer	B-7-1	95	272	699.10	675.00	7-23-35	1-23-36	
Ashcraft, Jesse	Ba-6.5	47.4	350	416.60	400.00	6-16-36	12-16-36	
Baker, Geo. M.	Ba-8-6	170.5	151	1526.28	1450.00	3-12-35	9-12-35	
Baker, Wilson	Ba-19-1	Ba-30-4a	149	70	1636.55	1490.00	12-6-34	6-6-35	
Bays, Aden	Mc-10-4	40	124	273.05	250.00	2-27-35	8-27-35	
Bays, Wiley	Mc-9-10	40	230	260.85	240.00	5-18-35	11-18-35	
Board, Nelle B.	B-21-1	Ba-2a	172	186	1296.57	1285.00	13-14-35	9-14-35	
Boling, Zack	Mc-28-5	80	243	726.85	680.00	5-3-35	11-3-35	
Borders, Ray Ba-13-3	Ba-14-4a	196	146	1517.93	1391.60	5-25-35	11-25-35	
Branson, Ida	Ba-30-1	Ba-19-7a	94	71	956.00	940.00	11-1-34	5-1-35	
Brassine, Severin	B-14-2	141	3	982.10	980.00	2-2-35	8-2-35	
Brock, Sherman Ba-19-2, 20:3a, 20:3b	20-3c	136	72	1256.45	1256.00	12-7-34	6-7-35	
Buchanan, Belle	M-5-1a	230	73	2322.60	2910.00	12-7-34	6-7-35	
Bynum, Samuel	Ba-32-2	Ba-8-5	60	265	203.40	198.00	4-11-35	10-11-35	
Belcher, John	Mc-17-7	100	296	602.50	565.00	7-1-35	1-1-36	
Belle, Emma	Ba-26-7	114	285	791.24	710.00	7-8-35	1-8-36	
Blake, Damon	Ba-31-2	400	250	364.59	334.00	7-20-35	1-20-36	
Brinkmeyer, Fred U.	Ba-35-7	160	279	1399.09	1320.00	4-14-35	9-14-35	
Brooks, John H.	Ba-31-1a	60	309	624.33	600.00	8-17-35	2-17-36	
Brock, Paul	Ba-32-1	Mc-36-1	80	291	355.92	320.00	7-13-35	1-13-36	
Brownell, Kenneth Y. Mc-13-7	Ba-15-7a	338	274	2432.71	2300.00	6-4-35	12-4-35	
(Peoples Nat. Bank-Sullivan, Ind.)								
Barnes, Liston	Mc-33-5	155	331	1549.35	1550.00	12-27-35	6-27-36	
Callahan, Ellen Waggoner Mc-15-11	Mc-10-3a	50	210	243.75	225.00	4-6-35	10-6-35	

Detail from a Resettlement Administration Project chart keyed to the plat map and indicating the status of land acquisition from those who are to be resettled.
Original Size of Chart 40" x 27⁷/₈"

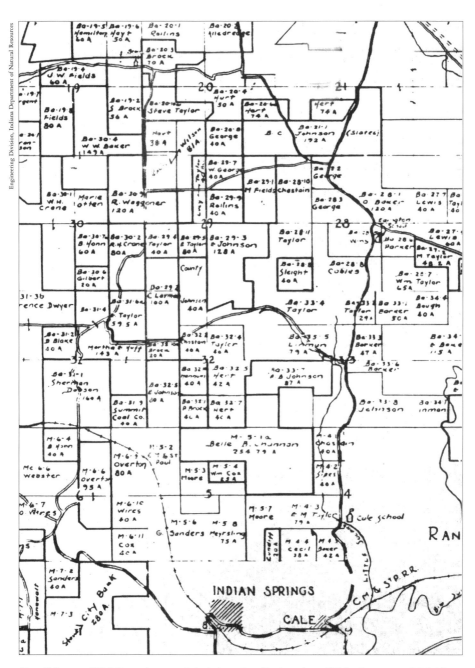

Detail from a 1935 Resettlement Administration Project Area IN-3 plat map, which iden-
tifies all landowners. Original Size of Map 33^{13}/$_{16}$" x 27^{15}/$_{16}$"

property was appraised for $1,057.75 on July 27, 1936, and purchased for $1,500.00. Condemnation was never used on the project.

Larger parcels were purchased as well. Eleven properties totaling 960 acres were acquired through tax delinquencies. This resulted in reimbursing $17,000 to Martin County. Other large acreages included Edmond Coady, 640 acres; John Spahr, 560 acres; Lawrence Dwyer, 498 acres; John Arnold, 480 acres; and W. S. Collins, 428 acres. Peoples National Bank of Sullivan was involved in the assumption of the Kenneth Brownell property containing 338 acres. State Life Insurance Company and Indianapolis Life Insurance sold 471 and 228 acres, respectively.

The project area price per acre varied from $3 to an exception with good improvements for $21.70. Otherwise, a few better farms sold for $10 to $14 per acre. However, most were valued from $5 to $10 per acre. Some properties in Martin County State Forest had some improvements on predominantly cutover land; by June 30, 1940, the 2,234 acres purchased averaged only $3.69 per acre. In comparison, the prices paid for tracts on the project appeared to be reasonable for that period of time.

RESETTLEMENT ADMINISTRATION

The Resettlement Administration was created in May 1935 to improve substandard urban and rural living conditions. Its first director was Rexford Tugwell, one of the early "New Deal brain-trusters." Because the Agriculture Adjustment Administration was not in the position of resettling people or developing areas, the Resettlement Administration, a new separate agency, took on this function, especially in rural communities. The Works Progress Administration provided labor. In fact, in Indiana the Resettlement Administration developed only the two state forest areas in Martin and Brown counties, while other welfare agencies developed the Ripley and Pulaski counties submarginal areas for state parks.

The Resettlement Administration immediately organized its central office in Washington, D.C. The agency then divided the nation into regions to properly administer developing areas and resettling people. Primarily agriculturists, foresters, and engineers were hired to develop areas; persons with social science backgrounds were assigned to resettling families. The Rehabilitation Section of the Resettlement Administration handled the movement of people out of the two new state forest areas. Personnel from the regional office handled this socialistic activity in Martin and Brown counties.

Those who had sold their properties were contacted and offered four different options regarding resettlement. One option involved moving and seeking other employment. Few made this choice. Option two provided aid in relocating to better farmland with equal or better buildings and improvements. Some people requested help, while others made their own selections. These families continued to farm. Many sellers used the third option. They either bought or rented other properties nearby, but outside of the boundaries of the purchase area, or they moved into a fifteen-unit housing complex, known as "Scenic Hill," built on the first hill east of Loogootee along the south side of U.S. 50 and U.S. 150. Local critics sometimes called it "Hitlerville." Sellers who used these three options were also eligible for low interest loans and employment on the project.

Option four permitted families to be placed on a list of people who were eligible to be relocated to a new communal community. The Resettlement Administration offered this option in 1937; soon after, it was terminated, and Tugwell had left federal employment. The Farm Security Administration (FSA), which was created after the passage of the Jones-Bankhead Farm Tenant Act of 1937, took over this activity. The FSA took responsibility for cooperative farms and continuation of the past land development operations of the Resettlement Administration.

Deshee Farm, Knox County

The history of Deshee Farm south of Vincennes, Knox County, provides a good example of this type of rehabilitation. J. Rebecca Thompson has documented Deshee Farm from its beginning to liquidation. Robert L. Reid's book *Back Home Again: Indiana in the Farm Security Administration Photographs, 1936–1943* uses photographs taken by the Farm Security Administration to illustrate the movement and activities of some families on this communal farm, as well as work done on the Martin County project.

The federal government acquired 2,771 acres in six scattered tracts; this became known as Wabash Farms. Deshee Farm, a component of Wabash Farms, consisted of several tracts, the two largest known as 41 and Beal Site, which was seven miles distant with smaller farms between them. Selected farms had a total of forty-two dwellings, nine barns, three milking sheds, and ten poultry houses. As many as forty-one families could live in the cooperative at any one time. In 1938, there were twenty-two families designated as members; there were thirty-

· eight by 1941, but that number dwindled to twenty-eight a year later. The cooperative never reached full capacity.

When operation of the farm began in 1938, the FSA provided housing, buildings, farming equipment, livestock, and other requirements for this farming venture. The farm was incorporated under state laws with the members as shareholders. A male in each family represented one member who could also run for election on the board of directors. The federal government held title to the property and employed a farm manager. The farm manager, who was also on the board, assigned each member to a specific operation, such as the dairy herd. An hourly time record was maintained for each member in order to determine his share of profits at the end of the year.

Deshee Farm had eighty-six farm members during its seven years in operation. One-fourth of them remained less than one year. As prosperity improved during the war years, many found other employment with better pay. Two-thirds stayed for less than one-half of the entire period, and only two members remained for seven years. Some conflicts existed between different membership groups. There were also management recommendations by higher officials that conflicted with local managers who had a better understanding of existing problems. Another

Children playing near one of the new homes in Wabash Farms project. Photograph taken in June 1938.

Library of Congress, Prints & Photographs Division, FSA/OWI Collection, LC-USF34-060999-D

These farmers are planting cantaloupes on Wabash Farms, Deshee Farm, May 1940.

communal idea had been tried at New Harmony, Indiana, a century before and failed. It had a "higher" society than the Wabash Farms project, but the two were beset by many of the same problems.

Congress began hearings about this communal activity soon after it began the socialistic experiment that critics called "Little Russia." Pressure for the Farm Security Administration to terminate federal ownership increased over a seven-year period. The last meeting of the board of directors of Deshee Farm was held on March 12, 1945, and public sales were held for the two large units and other scattered ones. Tract 41 became Schenk Sod Company in Knox County. Five members purchased tracts. Similar public sales were made of the homes at Scenic Hill in Martin County

Resettlement Administration Regional Office

R. C. Smith, as regional director, administered both rehabilitation and development of areas. Originally located in Urbana, Illinois, Smith came to Indianapolis when the office was moved to a location on Massachusetts Avenue. L. E. (Buck) Sawyer became development director, with Ralph F. Wilcox, a former Indiana state

Library of Congress, Prints & Photographs Division, FSA/OWI Collection, LC-USF34-060971-D

Some Martin County families were resettled to the Deshee Farm, which is now Schenk Sod Company, Vincennes. Photograph taken in May 1940.

forester, assistant director. Other officials were Raymond E. Kroodsma, chief forester, Samuel Sapirie, chief engineer, Eugene Boucher, landscape architect, and Herbert Allee, heavy equipment supervisor. I do not recall the names of persons in the rehabilitation section. There were ten such land use demonstration areas being developed in five midwestern states. Two each were in Illinois, Ohio, and Indiana. I believe two each were also in Iowa and Minnesota in this region. The two development projects in Indiana were more closely associated with those in Illinois and Ohio. Each individual project was under the direct supervision of the regional office.

Land Utilization Project/Shoals LU3

The names of the land utilization projects often represented some natural feature or locality, such as the White River Land Utilization Project. However, the Resettlement Administration's official designation for this project was Resettlement Administration, Land Utilization Division, Shoals LU3. In March 1935, James W. Pendry was appointed project manager. Land acquisition had progressed well with a reported 27,000 acres being optioned by June 30, 1935. There were enough tracts to warrant initial development. During the summer, Pendry began interviewing personnel, including a project forester and project engineer as his two assistants, as well as óthers. It was my good fortune to be selected project forester with Paul Swanson as my assistant.

William Wells served as project engineer with Gayle Kemp as assistant. I do not know about all of the past qualifications and experiences of all selected to administer the project. However, Pendry had been a county agricultural agent at Ravenna, Ohio. My forestry training included three years at Pennsylvania State Forest School and one year at North Carolina State University where I received a Bachelor of Science degree in forestry in 1930. I then worked as a forest ranger and nurseryman for the Florida Forest Service. Paul Swanson had attended the same school in Pennsylvania. I do not have any information about William Wells. Gayle Kemp graduated from Purdue University. Leonard Pickett obtained his engineering degree from Illinois University at a later date. During the Great Depression, the conservation of our natural resources became a high priority. There was a great demand for professionals with college degrees in these fields of expertise. My salary of $2,700 per annum was quite sufficient for the time.

It was a beautiful day on October 1, 1935, when I reported for duty. The Shoals office was located above the Herschel Woods Restaurant next to the Baltimore and Ohio Railroad. Diagonally across the tracks stood a large frame house known as the Wallace Hotel, which had probably offered overnight lodging to traveling salesmen during the horse and buggy days. However, Paul Swanson and I rented rooms at the residence of the Charles Runyon family. It was on Main Street and back of the Greyhound Bus Station lunch stop on U.S. Highways 50 and 150. Both of us were unmarried, so we alternated meals between the bus station's cafeteria and Herschel Woods Restaurant.

Considerable time was initially given to the hiring of experienced persons to supervise work in the field. There were three supervisors for forestry activities: William C. Seng, a former timber buyer and sawmill operator; William Payton, a timber appraiser and buyer; and Harry Dickerson, a foreman at the closed Loogootee CCC camp. In addition, Darell Martin, an outstanding CCC enrollee, was assigned to inspect purchased farms and to map areas for erosion control, tree planting, timber stand improvement, and other cultural practices.

Engineers supervised work on roads, buildings, and later dams. Walter Van Hoy, who had highway construction experience, was assigned to roadwork. Omer

Van Hoy was a master carpenter, and Audrene "Doc" Crim was an electrician. Harry Gerkin supervised heavy equipment operations. All were residents of Martin County. Lawrence Bauer, Clarence Ash, John Gootee, Dale Grindstaff, Porter Girdly, Ernest Sargent, Hayden Ritchey, Patrick Dwyer, Peter Risacher, and Sherman Pruitt assisted in various engineering activities.

All of this activity required a considerable office force. At Shoals, attorney James Snodgrass later joined Ralph Seals. Mrs. Ester Ketchum was their secretary. After transferring from land acquisition under Russell Otten, Lois Earl became secretary for Mr. Pendry. The pool of clerk-stenographers included Elizabeth Brown, Amelia Matthews, Katherine Grannon, and Betty Patterson. All were unmarried at that time and lived in Martin County. James VanMeter was a trained draftsman, and Clare Breidenbaugh investigated Works Progress Administration welfare applicants. Engineering and forestry personnel also occupied additional space in the office. Funds for employment came from the Resettlement Administration. It is of interest to note that all key persons in our office, including clerks, received notices of assignment from Washington, D.C., and were required to take the oath of office. In fact, an FBI agent spent several days at Shoals interviewing upper level personnel who were also fingerprinted.

The Shoals LU3 office of the Resettlement Administration occupied the upper stories of this building from the fall of 1935 to summer 1936.

Our annual budget required itemizing estimated expenditures for each work activity, such as tree planting. The budget included man-days, equipment, materials, supplies, and other costs along with a 10 percent contingency. In the fall and winter of 1935 and 1936, office staff hired and instructed personnel and spent time learning purchasing procedures and federal regulations for operation. Purchases for forestry work included trucks, hand tools for tree planting, timber stand improvement, and forest fire suppression, as well as seedlings for spring plantings and many other miscellaneous supplies. The engineering section, of course, had to acquire heavy equipment along with a wide variety of tools and materials for construction.

Obviously, this required many days in the office preparing requisitions. Each item required considerable detail to insure against inferior substitutes. Several wholesale outlets provided the necessary information. Catalogues issued by Van Camp and Vonnegut Hardware Companies in Indianapolis and Belknap Hardware in Louisville, Kentucky, provided a ready source for competitive bidding. All requisitions were processed through the Resettlement Administration office in Indianapolis; we had limited authority for petty cash purchases for emergency purposes only.

When it was necessary to use a personal automobile, detailed mileage readings from point to point were required. If the typist made any erasures on the travel voucher, it was necessary to place your initials above each one.

Labor Force, Works Progress Administration (WPA)

The WPA operated over all of Martin County. When the U.S. Department of Agriculture was acquiring the area for the state forest in 1934, it was assumed that the WPA would be furnishing all of the labor for development. However, in 1935 when the Resettlement Administration focused on rehabilitation, landowners who optioned their farms were given employment regardless of financial status. This also applied to administrative personnel jobs. During peak employment periods, this project utilized around 700 people.

The WPA operated in other parts of the county as well. It built small lakes and ponds on private properties where owners agreed to permit fishing by the public. Another activity involved building outdoor privies. A standard construction form was used to pour a concrete stool and floor with an attached pipe and wood framed closet. Road and street repair jobs were also popular activities in 1933 and 1934.

There were many sources of labor. During the depression, many unemployed persons were wandering the streets in large cities. A tent camp, for temporary use by such men, was set up on an acquired farm in Baker Township. During that same period, the CCC camp in Loogootee was being phased out after construction was completed on the Martin County State Forest. This made it possible to move the transients into the buildings formerly used by the CCC enrollees. Transportation to work sites was provided by similar flatbed trucks used by the CCC. At a later date, a new work camp was constructed at a more central location in order to relieve this travel problem. All other workers, including supervisory and office personnel, provided their own transportation. Project rolling stock remained at major work sites or at designated parking lots and was identified with decals on each door. Most of the men from the work camp were assigned to construct buildings, roads, and the Lake Greenwood dam.

Another source of labor became available when area landowners, who sold their properties, became eligible for employment. Those who did not sell could also work if they were approved for welfare. Both of these groups were farmers who made good workers on forestry crews. WPA workers, mostly from Martin County, were also transferred from leaf raking jobs to more meaningful employment on the project.

Three forestry field supervisors organized crews with approximately twenty men each. A foreman was selected to oversee each crew with priority being given to residents of the area. Many proved to be outstanding workers; they quickly learned the importance of forestry and other conservation practices. Will Ritchey, James Brock, Fay Harris, Alva Swayzee, Wilson Baker, and Thurman Jones were among those chosen.

Engineering crews did not necessarily follow the organization described above. One of their first actions concerned the building and repair of roads. Crushed limestone was first hauled in from a long distance until a deposit of limestone was discovered near Sargent's Store in McCameron Township. After the acquisition of a stone crusher, Charles Chastain was hired to operate the small quarry. Surveying crews also laid out new roads and settled any property line disputes.

Erosion control and timber stand improvement began as soon as equipment and tools became available in the first winter of 1935–1936. Plans were made for forestry work by using soil survey maps, aerial photographs, and U.S. Geological Survey Quadrangles. These maps were also used to record each completed activity, such as number and species of trees planted, acreage of timber stand improvement, and such.

By the spring and summer of 1936, engineering projects were in full swing with several hundred workers. The site for a dam had been found, and construction on it, as well as on several new buildings, was initiated. Tree planting, timber stand improvement, erosion control, water hole construction, establishment of wildlife refuges, and planting of wildlife food and cover plots began. During the summer of 1936, a severe drought occurred with record high temperatures; above 100 degrees Fahrenheit in July caused considerable discomfort for the workers. An all time high of 114 degrees occurred on July 14. Salt pills were given to laborers in the field along with early dismissal on a few days.

Burns City LU3

The name of the project changed from Shoals LU3 to Burns City LU3 when the office was moved. It had become evident that the Shoals office should be more centrally located. In September 1936, a move was made to a farmstead on the west side of State Highway 45 in McCameron Township. The farmstead contained a one-story frame house with several rooms and a large barn with a small spring behind it. Another building, a short distance downhill, served as a tool house. Desks and other office equipment were set up in different rooms. A concrete walk led to an outside pit toilet. Everyone brought their own lunch, and one of the men used his carryall van to transport the women from their homes in Shoals and Loogootee at a round trip cost of 25 cents per day. The barn, located back of the office, also stabled two riding horses, John and Joe. Because of bad roads and long walking distances, especially to forestry sites, it was reasoned that they were needed. On an area covering three townships, I personally found that a pickup truck and walking were much faster.

The work force greatly increased. Some former employees had resigned, while new ones came on, including Leonard Pickett, assistant project engineer; Bert Stevenson, a new engineer; Keith Dustin, auditor; John Harmeling, office manager; Joseph Smith, clerk; Gerald Williams, chief timekeeper; Russell Roach, draftsman; and clerk stenographers Mary Lela Cushing, Cecilia Doyle, Lillian Brown, and Mildred Baker, all unmarried at that time. At a later date, William Wells transferred to another project at Crab Orchard in Southern Illinois, and

(Left to Right) Leonard Pickett, James Pendry, and William Barnes (the author) were employed on the project.

(Center) Cecilia Doyle, who later married the author, (Left) Katherine Grannon, and (Right) Mary Lela Cushing were project employees.

Leonard Pickett filled this vacancy. Alton Hawkins was in charge of assignment of WPA employees and payment of checks to them. Personnel remained the same with the exception that vacancies created by resignations were filled by Margaret Thompson, Katherine O'Brian, and Mrs. Naomi Brown.

One of the first lessons about our relocation to the country concerned the use of a standard telephone party line. It was no way to do business, as the click of receivers could be heard every time a call came through. This prompted our early request for a private line. The new headquarters functioned until a better office at the work camp was completed. The completed work camp, a short distance to the west, had one of the large barracks for office use. With the exception of a smaller room on one end, the remainder functioned as one long space with a section for each operating group.

An interesting incident took place in my office in the farmhouse while I was in the field. It involved my secretary, Cecilia Doyle, who later became my wife. She opened a drawer in a file cabinet and was greeted by a large pilot black snake that came slithering out. Cecilia ended up screaming on top of a nearby desk. Rescuers came running from the adjoining room, including two inspectors from

After September 1936, the Shoals unit of the Resettlement Administration moved to this new headquarters in the project area near Burns City.

the Indianapolis office. I do not know if they thought it was amusing. Paul Swanson had captured the snake, but evidently failed to secure the sack holding it.

Politics

No one inquired about my political affiliation. Likewise, I did not request that information from others. However, politics in Martin County was, and still is, a subject of great interest. At that time, William Jenner, who practiced law in Shoals, was a strong Republican and later became U.S. senator after moving to Lawrence County. Frank Gilkison in Shoals and Hugh Gray in Loogootee were county leaders for the same party. All were quite critical about the so-called boondoggle involving welfare expenditure for unemployed people. County offices were held by Democrats, with James Marshall the Democratic County Chair. Clare Breidenbaugh, Fabius Gwin, an old time lawyer in Shoals, and Sheriff Thomas Arvin were active in Democratic politics. (Clare investigated WPA applicants.) Requests were made for voluntary contributions to the party. During that period as well as during my ensuing thirty-seven years of public employment, I could not see the logic in managing our natural resources on a political basis. My advice to any subordinates under me has always been "to vote as your conscience dictates" and to "keep your nose out of politics." However, in the case of employment under the WPA, I do not recall that any local active Republicans received any favors on the project.

Public Relations

During the time our office was in Shoals, and later in the project area, our entire staff endeavored to maintain good public relations in the county. The employment of local people created a favorable attitude not only from an employment standpoint, but it also boosted the economy of all surrounding communities. We also became involved in the local community and spent time educating the public about our activities.

The importance of informing the public about the purposes and objectives of the project was the focus of considerable attention. Talks were given at conservation and service clubs. A registration box, containing information about preventing forest fires and a sheet for visitors to sign, was placed near the steps of the fire tower. Tours to the dam and future recreational uses of the lake, along with field inspections of tree planting, timber stand improvement, erosion control, and other development activities all contributed to a better understanding of this land utilization project. Robert Graham, who sponsored the Graham Farm Fair on his farm in Daviess County, provided a tent for display of a papier-mâché model of our area along with printed material explaining its objectives.

The U.S. Army Corps of Engineers had held a public meeting in the Shoals High School gymnasium to discuss flood control on the East Fork of White River, emphasizing a feasibility study that had been conducted. Extensive drill cores revealed the location of a site for a high dam on the Otway Baker farm above Shoals. An overflow crowd listened to a discussion of the objectives of the project: flood control, low flow augmentation, recreation, and fish and wildlife enhancement. The large reservoir would back water in Martin and Lawrence counties to the edge of Jackson County. A large number of landowners who attended the meeting objected to the loss of valuable farmland in the valley. Others were concerned about the hydroelectric plant at Williams and backing water into Spring Mill State Park. Some of our personnel attended but did not make any comments. The proposal for the reservoir was dropped after the meeting.

Homes and farms along U.S. Highway 150 were inundated by floodwaters in 1937; the White River Land Utilization Project helped provide relief.

An opportunity to serve the public arose during the 1937 flood, which created an urgent demand for relief. Thousands of acres of bottomland in Spencer County were inundated. The town of Leavenworth in Crawford County was damaged to such an extent that it was necessary to relocate it on a high hill.

The White River and its two forks also reached high levels. According to William Keller, whose family has kept weather records at Shoals for many years, this flood was around five feet lower than the Great Flood of 1913. The main highways and railroad grades remained above water. Homes in "Frog Eye" section of Shoals and along U.S. Highway 150 were also flooded. Water came up on the south end of Main Street just below Wilson Chenoweth's barn. Our drivers and trucks were dispatched to various localities, especially along the Ohio River.

Project Dedication

The White River Land Utilization Project was representative of a nationwide movement to purchase and retire submarginal areas from cultivation and devote them to forestry, fish and wildlife conservation, and recreation. It was an attempt

The "Frog Eye" section of Shoals, an area of lower ground, flooded in 1937.

to solve some of the deep-rooted land and social problems. Remedial objectives were to secure adjustments in small governmental units in order to retire county roads and consolidate schools. The project made a huge impact upon the people and the land of the area.

On September 15, 1939, the White River Land Utilization Project was dedicated at a ceremony held in the shelter house in the picnic area. A large crowd attended this event that was cooperatively sponsored by the U.S. Department of Agriculture, Soil Conservation Service, and Indiana Department of Conservation. Dillon S. Myer, representing the federal government, assistant chief of the Soil Conservation Service, gave the dedicatory address. James W. Pendry, project manager; A. M. Hedge, assistant to regional conservator of Soil Conservation Service; Kenneth Welton, acting regional conservator of Soil Conservation Service; and Phil G. Beck, regional director of Farm Security Administration, also participated in the dedication ceremony. State officials recognized "the project as a major contribution toward...future recreation and as an advancement of the conservation program in which more than four hundred thousand Hoosiers are actively participating."

The work camp office for the White River Land Utilization Project remained open until transfer to the Division of Forestry, Indiana Department of Conservation and termination of all employees on the entire project on June 30, 1940. In addition to the purchase of the land, the U.S. Department of Agriculture bore the expense for administering its development. The Resettlement Administration assumed jurisdiction in early 1935, but had only paid certain expenses until October 31, 1937. From that date until the end of the project, the project was under several agencies of the Agricultural Department. The land utilization division of the Farm Security Administration served from November 1, 1937 until June 30, 1938; the Bureau of Agricultural Economics from July 1, 1938 until October 1, 1938; and the Soil Conservation Service until its termination in 1940.

WORK PROJECTS

The chief objective of each forestry and engineering work project was meaningful work for all employees. The requests and desires of the Division of Forestry, Indiana Department of Conservation were followed to create a new state forest. This included the construction of buildings necessary for administration, as well as the conversion of the land into an area for future maximum production of forest products on a sustained yield basis. The public use of this state forest also mandated a provision for recreational use in equal proportion to the major objective of growing timber. Both uses were compatible with road access to picnic areas, trails, and other facilities. At the beginning of acquisition, we did not know that there was a location for impounding a large lake. This discovery enhanced the opportunity to create a major recreational area for the people of southwestern Indiana.

Lake Greenwood

The engineering section soon found a site on Furse Creek where it was possible to impound the water to create an 800-acre lake. At this place, a natural peninsula extended partway across the valley. An examination of a topographic map revealed a favorable ratio of ten acres of watershed to one surface acre of water. The Indiana Geological Survey at Indiana University assigned Dr. Ralph Esarey to conduct a feasibility study. Soil sample drillings revealed the peninsula to be composed of sandy material. An underground layer of blue silt above bedrock was found in the valley between the peninsula and the north hillside.

The geological history of the selected site dated back to Illinoian glaciation. When temperatures moderated and the glacier melted, it created a glacial lake that backed into the unglaciated hills at the edge of the drift area. Sand and gravel and other soil particles deposited by the glacier formed the peninsula, while the melt-water sediment left a deep layer of this blue silt in the valley. When water was added to this silty material, it became unstable, making it necessary to cut a wide, deep cutoff trench to be filled with clay soil.

Design plans for the dam required wood pilings cut on the project to be driven into the sandy portion on the south side before the concrete emergency spillway could be poured. In addition, a de-watering conduit on the bottom of the lake was placed in the northern fill section of the dam. Workers placed a rip-rap layer of large stones along the entire length of the dam. It extended above and below the waterline for reducing erosion by wave action.

"Cletracs" such as this one were used on the Lake Greenwood project.

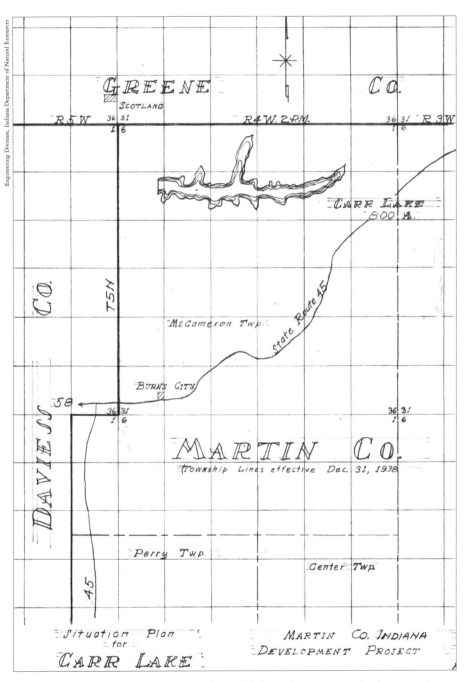

Carr Lake, later named Lake Greenwood, provided a unique opportunity for recreation.
Size of original "Situation Plan" 8 $^7/_{16}$" x 11"

An interesting event happened when construction started. Bids submitted for purchase of tractors had resulted in the award being given to Cleveland Tractor Company for Cletracs tractors. The Caterpillar Company claimed that its tractor, which cost more, was superior for pulling a scraper to haul fill material. Consequently, it provided a tractor to compete with a marked Cletrac, and a race was on. A tallyman recorded each trip as the two machines came down the hill on the north side. As I recall, daily counts made over a period of many days showed little difference between the two.

The forestry section had the joint obligation of sodding and seeding the dam. Sod was cut at old house sites by means of a horsedrawn wide plank with a steel cutting bar attached. Sodded strips on the contour held seeded areas between them. Another assignment required the clearing of 300 acres of timber and brush in the lake basin. Survey stakes and flagging markers were placed at intervals around the entire water line.

Clearing of the lakebed coincided with construction of the dam. All trees were cut flush with the ground out to a depth of six feet below the marked shoreline. Higher stumps were permitted past that line. Fish shelters were anchored to some of these stumps by fastening long poles that were staked in the ground at the other end. Brush was inserted under the circle of poles, and rectangular brush piles were also staked into the ground and held with wire. There were a total of 423 such shelters placed in the lake. Spawning beds were also made by hauling and spreading 2,194 cubic yards of crushed limestone from the shoreline out to a six-foot depth. After salvaged logs had been hauled away, it was necessary to burn all remaining green material. Old automobile tires obtained from many sources fed fires on a twenty-four-hour basis.

At the time of this activity, a serious problem existed. One of the landowners had not optioned his farm. As condemnation had not been approved, it became evident that negotiations for the property must receive priority. William Payton, in addition to his field supervision of forestry work, had been successful in optioning several tracts. He was assigned the task of contacting the holdout. J. W. Waggoner owned this last un-optioned 100-acre tract, where the boathouse, dock, small house, and public use area were to be located. His family had lived there for many years and had made a living raising farm crops and livestock. One of the Waggoners still hunted squirrels with a treeing dog and used a muzzle-loading gun. After Payton had spent many days talking with the owner, Waggoner signed an option making it possible to continue clearing the lake basin and to begin work on these other facilities.

In summary, Lake Greenwood was completed in the fall of 1937. It later reached a maximum depth of 40 feet. The total length at the top elevation of the dam measured 1,941 feet with a height of 55 feet. The lake extended from west to east for approximately four miles. With the inclusion of the largest embayment in Little Creek on the north side, the shoreline equaled 18.5 miles. It was usually referred to as 800 acres in size, while other reports listed it as 805 and 820 acres.

As work progressed, the question of naming the lake arose. The first name chosen was Carr Lake, as the 105-acre farm on which the dam was located had been owned by George Carr. However, further research revealed another natural lake in Kosciusko County with the same name. Congressman Arthur H. Greenwood from Washington, Indiana, had naturally shown great interest, as it was in his district. So, it was named in his honor. When a body of water is named for a man, his name usually precedes the word "lake." Over the years, the name has changed to Lake Greenwood, and it has been used thusly in this text.

Even if there had not been a person with that name, it would certainly have been an appropriate name, with the surrounding hills covered with green trees of the state forest. It was obviously of little political importance, as Congressman Greenwood lost in the 1938 election. Gerald Landis, his successor, visited the new lake after being elected to Congress.

It should be mentioned that other sites were studied as possible locations for impoundments. Another dam further downstream on Furse Creek would have created a much larger water area in Lake Greenwood by backing up another arm toward Culpepper School. The prohibition against the use of condemnation caused a problem with this site. Marion Porter, who owned 160 acres, forbade any acquisition person to set foot on his property, so no investigation of another dam site took place. My only contact with Porter occurred on a Saturday afternoon in November. Jim Snodgrass and I had decided to go quail hunting on the north side of the lake. We were crossing a cornfield in one corner of his property below the dam. Suddenly, Marion jumped out from the seclusion of a shock of corn. He began shouting and waving his arms and threatening us with arrest. We made a very rapid exit with guns and dogs. Several years later, I learned about his removal from a friend living near our home in Indianapolis. Julius Weicher, a retired federal marshal, told about his encounter with Mr. Porter when the U.S. Navy was acquiring the area. He found Marion away from his house and peaceably accompanied him off the property after identifying himself and displaying his badge.

Public Use Area

The engineering project required the construction of an access road, picnic area, boathouse, and custodian's cottage as a public use complex for the future state forest. The new, surfaced road meandered downhill from its connection with State Highway 45. An opening in the woods and an old overgrown field offered a view of the upper end of Lake Greenwood. The road then passed above the boathouse into a parking lot for the picnic area. From there, it continued to a boat launching area for use by private boats.

The picnic area on a side hill contained a large shelter house. This timber and sandstone structure contained four fireplaces. Two faced the interior. One of the two exterior fireplaces had a firebox with a cooking surface. The interior floor and adjoining sides were made of this same native sandstone, and heavy squared-timber supports complemented this natural design. All of the materials came from the sawmill and from wells and foundations salvaged from home sites. The roof, covered with white oak shakes, split by two local workers who still had froes for making hand-split shakes, further enhanced the structure's appearance. The shelter house and adjoining grounds had sturdy picnic tables. The ones outside were placed on large sandstone slabs and anchored to steel rods driven into the ground to prevent movement. The picnic area also extended over the hill back of the large shelter house. A path led from it to a secluded spot where a small shelter was built with logs and sandstone. It became a favorite place for small groups. Pit toilets provided sanitary facilities.

The boathouse, like all other structures in the public use area, was constructed with native hardwood lumber. It was located on a point where an embayment met the main lake. Square oak piling supported the pier with separate compartments for rental boats. The building provided space for storage and sale of outboard motors, fishing equipment, and other items. Fishing licenses were also sold along with live bait and snacks when the area opened. A utility line later provided electricity for lighting in the entire public use area as well as for operation of a deep well pump for water.

Other Buildings

The Indiana Division of Forestry, in its original responsibility to administer this future state forest, had requested residences for a forest superintendent and a district forester for southwestern Indiana, along with a service building and barn for the area. The state also appointed a person to operate the concession at the boathouse. The contract required the concessionaire to return 20 percent of the income to the state. A small four-room house was built for his occupancy during the summer season. It stood on a high bank on the embayment south of the boathouse.

The home for the forest superintendent was located on the same ridge south of the farmstead office. This frame building was constructed of native lumber from the sawmill and had exterior horizontal siding of one-inch, air-dried boards. These boards had a straight edge on the inside while the bark remained on the exposed unedged outside. The application of brown stain produced a rustic appearance that blended with the adjoining landscape. Kiln-dried tulip poplar boards gave a pleasing effect to all interior walls. Purchases were made of other finishing materials to complete the design.

This house on Lake Greenwood served as a home for Bill Barnes and his family starting in the fall of 1939. This picture shows the snow-bound house in late December of that year.

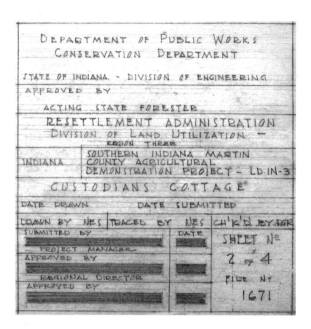

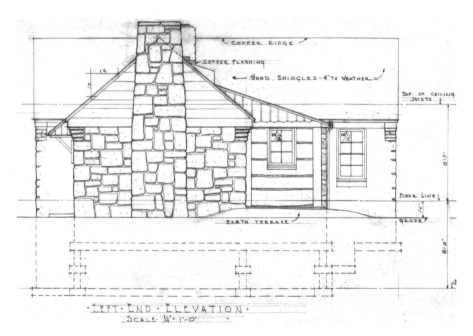

LEFT·END·ELEVATION·
SCALE 1/4"·1'-0"

Details from the architectural drawings for the custodian's cottage; the left-end elevation above illustrates design elements used throughout the project area. Bill and Cecilia Barnes lived in this house. Size of original drawing 24" x 35⁷/₈"

The residence for the district forester was more pretentious than the other buildings with its location on a hill above the south side of the dam. The exterior of native sandstone enhanced its appearance. The service building was a frame structure used for an office, workshop, and space for repair of motorized equipment. The barn, later called the "mule barn," was located on a hill near the dam.

At the time our office moved from Shoals, plans were also made for building a 200-man work camp near the old office location. Construction included a series of barracks, office building, mess hall, pump house, and water tank. A deep well provided necessary water for drinking and sanitary requirements. One building had separate partitions for small rooms, while the others were open for rows of single beds. The bill of materials for lumber to be furnished by the sawmill far exceeded the requirements for all other structures. This included all framing lumber for inside and outside construction. Other sources were required for shingles, flooring, inside walls, windows, doors, and trim. The exterior walls had rough-sawn boards painted with brown stain to give a rustic appearance. Due to the rolling ground, most buildings sat on foundation pilings.

The new camp was occupied in the winter of 1937–1938, and our office moved into its new quarters in mid–April 1938. One long, large room served as office space for all service personnel, while two small rooms at its end provided offices for attorneys and project manager staff. The old farmhouse soon disappeared, but the barn remained for stabling the horses.

Telephone communication was poor when the project started and further deteriorated with the removal of farm families. It soon became necessary to change and maintain lines for local and long distance calls. The main line ran to Shoals by way of Dover Hill. As local maintenance was inadequate, the project became responsible for maintenance of twenty-seven miles of line. Project workers also installed necessary utility lines, as electricity had not been available for rural residents until the rural electrification program of the New Deal.

Obliteration of Buildings

Buildings and other improvements on acquired properties were demolished. Most were too poor quality for public sale, but the project salvaged and utilized any good material. On one occasion when V. M. Simmons, commissioner of the Indiana Department of Conservation, visited the project, he was asked about the disposal of an above-average bungalow. His reply was: "Tear it down as someone will want to live in it and require maintenance in the future."

Unsalvageable material could be bulldozed into a pile and burned during winter, or in the summer when there was no danger of spreading fire. All basements and wells were filled in after removal of top layers of flat sandstone needed for other construction purposes. This action eliminated potential hazards to man or wildlife that might fall into the deep holes. This work required the razing of 811 buildings and the filling of 300 wells.

Roads

The construction of new roads and the repair and maintenance of old ones were ongoing activities during the entire development period. After the opening of the limestone quarry, this material was in ample supply for use. Most of the eight miles of new construction took place on the south side of Lake Greenwood for access to the dam on the west end and to the public use area on the east end, as well as for connections with buildings and other facilities. Another seven miles of existing roads were repaired as needed for travel by workers from Shoals and other directions. In total, workers built 100 culverts and six bridges for these roads.

Forestry Projects

Inspections of purchased land showed both gully and sheet erosion on abandoned fields and serious losses of soil on cropland. Some landowners had not been too particular about farming on the contour, especially on steeper slopes. The new Soil Conservation Service was just beginning to recommend soil conservation practices using grass strips on the contour and sodded waterways. Erosion control on newly purchased tracts began during the winter of 1935–1936 and continued during the life of the project. Methods for controlling erosion have already been described under the CCC program. However, the flat rocks, timbers, poles, salvaged boards, and heavier items from obliterated farmsteads were used to build these dams.

Immediate action had to be taken to prevent further loss of topsoil on newly acquired cropland. Beginning in February 1936, every open field was seeded with Korean lespedeza. This imported species had been recently introduced for seeding on acid soils and proved to be better than the smaller and more procumbent Japanese lespedeza. *Lespedeza sericea* also came on the market about the same time. It grew higher, but would not spread well. So, tons of Korean lespedeza seed were bought for use on acquired tracts.

Sawmill

As previously explained, the engineering section had an early demand for all types of construction material. William Seng, one of our forestry supervisors, had experience in sawmill operation. Consequently, the project procured a new portable sawmill, logging truck, and other necessary equipment. The mill was set up in Turkey Creek Valley below Sargent's Store in McCameron Township. Although all of the wooded tracts had been cut over, enough good quality timber remained in scattered stands.

Various species of oaks provided the bulk of heavy timbers needed for piers, the shelter house, and foundation material. One-inch, oak boards of various widths were rough sawn for exterior siding. Thicker material for studs, rafters, and other unexposed surfaces came from oak, tulip poplar, sycamore, elm, and ash. It was air dried for several weeks. Due to higher moisture content, some of the oak exterior siding split and cracked. Mr. Combs, who had run a sawmill in Greene County, operated the mill. A young Purdue forestry graduate graded and filled orders.

Timber Stand Improvement

The major objective in the management of all state forests was the production of high quality trees in accordance with the capability of each forest type at each site. Growing conditions varied due to direction and steepness of slopes, moisture fluctuations, and quality of soil. Thus, timber stand improvement became an important forest conservation measure over the entire area.

Forest conditions in the project area were similar to those in many parts of Indiana. Economic need had resulted in the cutting of timber. In fact, many trees with potentially high values had been cut for cross ties. At one place, young black walnuts had even been used for fence posts. Second-growth stands had many unmerchantable trees that resulted from past high-grading practices. Many had stump rot resulting from forest fires or diseases. Others were crooked or had double forks. Woodlot grazing left little understory reproduction.

Timber stand improvement became an important activity that provided labor during all periods of the year. Fortunately, our work crews were composed of those skilled in the use of the axe and crosscut saw. Our supervisory personnel spent considerable time and effort teaching the fundamental functions of good forest management. Each crew had about twenty men under one foreman. The foreman was usually a local farmer, as were most members of the crew. They provided their own transportation to work sites. The foreman also kept time and maintained the necessary Red Cross safety kit. Another person sharpened axes and crosscut saws. A five-gallon oak keg with a spigot was filled with cold water and wrapped with wet burlap to keep it cool for workers' consumption.

Cultural practices varied in accordance with forest types. The beech-maple type grew on some slopes. Large defective beech (wolf trees) occupied considerable growing spaces and inhibited reproduction beneath them. These were girdled rather than cut. We also followed this procedure with other defective species. Preference was given to oaks, sugar maple, tulip poplar, and the like. Where these trees, especially the oaks, had multiple trunks, they were reduced to the dominant one. Each cut was sloped away from the remaining stem in order to prevent water rot in the cut. Competing inferior species were girdled or cut. Where possible, we felled the trees on the contour in order to catch leaves on the forest floor and retain moisture. Some limbs were lopped to encourage early reproduction. Grape vines were cut at ground level, except those on a small strip of woodland bordering open land were left for wildlife use.

The oak-hickory forest type grew on ridge tops and upper slopes. Level areas and north and east facing slopes with better moisture supported white and black oaks associated with pignut and small-fruited hickories. Drier ridges and west and south facing slopes had slower growing post, black, and scarlet oaks mixed with pignut and mockernut hickories. Timber stand improvement favored the oaks. In fact, the general rule for all of this work on different forest types downgraded species with lower market values like elm, beech, and all of the hickories.

Some lower northern slopes, as well as those facing the east with good moisture contents, supported mixed mesophytic stands of shagbark and bitternut hickories, white and red oaks, tulip poplar, white ash, and elms. There was an occasional black walnut or wild black cherry, along with beech and hard maple. Future crop trees were selected in accordance with their forms and growing conditions. Beech, black gum, and hickories were not favored.

With the exception of Furse Creek Valley back of the dam, land acquisition had been concentrated on cheaper tracts above valleys. However, some farms contained bottomlands. Farmers had cleared many of the valleys in the upper reaches of Boggs, Turkey, and Sulphur creeks where they were wide enough for a few rows of corn. The others, with tree species similar to those on adjoining lower slopes, received the same cultural treatment. However, there were a greater number of faster growing tulip poplar, red oak, and black walnut trees to be favored. This composition changed as valleys widened downstream. Some uncleared areas with poor drainage and a higher water table still contained timber. Pin oak, swamp white oak, and sycamore were favored over river birch, silver maple, box elder, and willow.

Some cleared fields had been abandoned for many years. They again supported closed canopies of young tulip poplar, elm, ash, and other species primarily of wind-blown origin. Tulip poplars, in particular, were several inches in diameter. Later a grid system using sixteen-feet centers was developed for selecting trees that should be favored. Workers eliminated competing species, but not to the extent where sassafras and other nurse crop trees permitted the selected species to become "limby." This method did not require much labor.

As previously mentioned, timber stand improvement became a major activity during the entire development era. It utilized meaningful labor in all seasons. The summer of 1936 was dry and hot, and a few days the temperature exceeded 100 degrees Fahrenheit. Leaves on some trees turned yellow in August. Conversely, the winter of 1939–1940 had temperatures below zero. Other than these stressful periods, work progressed very well. Around 13,000 acres of forested land were covered by the end of the project.

Timber Cruise

Good forestry practices mandated a forest inventory. It differed from a typical yearly business inventory in that the times between these counts were much longer due to the slow growth of the "product." Subsequent sample plots would be used to collect more data on growth. This forest survey was initiated after timber stand improvement had progressed to the point where measurements of the remaining standing trees could be taken. At that time, the usual method utilized a 10 percent cruise of timber on each tract. The inventory area covered a width of one-half chain on each side of the centerline. These parallel strips were ten chains apart. Workers on the timber cruise were selected in accordance with their ability to identify trees. A forestry graduate from Purdue University made this survey.

Tree Planting

The organization of tree planting crews followed the same procedure as previously described under timber stand improvement. However, the equipment simply required planting bars and buckets. Shovels were used for heeling-in seedlings needed for each planting site. During the early CCC days, the Division of Forestry had given instructions on the use of a grub hoe for digging the hole for each plant. I found this to be very slow and soon changed to a planting bar. It was the standard implement used in Florida and doubled the number of seedlings that could be planted in one day. This three-foot iron bar, with a cross handle and chisel-shaped blade, could be quickly inserted into the soil. It was especially good for planting hardwood seedlings with taproots.

Two men were assigned to each row. The one with the planting bar adjusted his two steps for placing seedlings at six-foot intervals. The other man carried the plants in a partially filled bucket of water and inserted the seedling in each hole before it was closed with the bar. This spacing interval for conifers and hardwoods required around 1,200 trees per acre. Many of these trees eventually died but the close spacing resulted in clearer trunks of surviving ones.

In order to reduce weed competition, local farmers using horse-drawn plows worked on an hourly basis to make contour furrows on planting sites. They became quite adept at placing them on level six-foot row intervals. This aided in holding water runoff, as well as eliminating the need for scalping vegetation around each hole.

Pine Plantations

White, red, pitch, shortleaf, jack, Scotch, and Virginia pines were available species. Three of the pines were native to Indiana. Charles C. Deam's *Trees of Indiana* (1932) reported that jack pine was originally found close to Lake Michigan in the three counties that border the lake. The range of white pine extended from this lake into isolated cool spots in northwestern Indiana as far south as Sugar Creek in Montgomery County. Virginia pine grew in four counties in the Knobstone escarpment in the southern part of the Norman Upland. Pitch pine primarily grew in mountainous areas in the eastern United States. The range of shortleaf pine was south of Indiana. Scotch pine was introduced from Europe.

My first preference was white pine followed by red, Virginia, pitch, Scotch, and jack pines. There were reasons to select or reject some species aside from their existing availability. Earlier plantings of white pine showed superior quality, and their native range was north of the project area. Red pine was the usual species in mixed plantations with white pine. Virginia pine grew on poor sites and could spread into old fields and eroded sites. Pitch pine was an additional species used in mixed pine plantations. Early Scotch pine plantations in Pennsylvania had shown good prospects until it was found that they were susceptible to wind storms and damage by yellow-bellied sapsuckers. Limited numbers of Scotch pine as well as jack pine were planted on the project area. Both were poor substitutes for Virginia pine.

Shortleaf pine was rejected because of its more southern range. However, the U.S. Forest Service favored it. It may have been more resistant to fires, but I believed it to be subject to winter-kill. A few experimental plantings of loblolly pine were also made elsewhere, but this species was rejected because of its southern range.

Most plantations had from two to four different kinds of trees. This reduced the danger of some future disease or insect infestation that might destroy plantations. At that time, there was some apprehension concerning white pine blister rust. The Division of Forestry endeavored to eliminate the host, Ribes (black currant), over the entire state. This practice was later terminated as a means for controlling this disease. The existence of Ribes was never a serious threat, especially in the unglaciated region where this host plant was uncommon.

Pine plantations on the better sites contained white pine mixed with either red or pitch pine. A few others had Virginia or Scotch pine added to these combinations. Eroded fields were planted with Scotch, jack, or Virginia pines above gullies, with Virginia pine given preference and scattered among black locust for future reseeding purposes. With the exception of a few scattered conifers, eroded areas were planted with one-year-old, black locust seedlings. They were placed at close intervals around the sides of active gullies. Black locust was also planted in contour furrows on sheet erosion above them. Most of the stock used during the 1936 and 1937 planting seasons came from the Clark County State Nursery. With the exception of black locust seedlings and black walnuts sold by the bushel, the supply was limited to conifers. These were grown for two years as 2-0 stock. No transplants were requisitioned. White pine was the desired species for better sites with red pine or pitch pine as the second choice in mixtures with white pine. Some areas had two or three rows of these mixtures bordering hardwood plantations. This helped to reduce the drying effects of winds. In 1936 and 1937, and to a certain extent during all of the development period, it was necessary to rely on the state nursery for planting stock. This also included 1,000 bald cypress placed along the north shoreline of Lake Greenwood.

The Division of Forestry recommended the use of pines to prepare sites for future invasion by native hardwoods. I was dubious of the philosophy of using only conifers; I considered jack and Scotch pines to be of inferior quality. I believed that closed canopies in a pine plantation with dry needles on the shaded forest floor would retard invasion of hardwoods. Many open areas, with sassafras, dogwood, sumac, and other nurse species, would also re-seed with tulip poplar, ashes, and maples along with oaks near bordering woods. If broom sedge grass had not created dense stands in such open areas, natural reproduction of hardwoods would be faster. broom sedge grass competition could be controlled by contour-plowed rows for seedlings.

Good forestry practices could not wait for the original forest types to be reestablished. On cleared fields some of the native hardwoods, like tulip poplar, were better substitutes than conifers. The reversion of open fields to forest cover involved a difficult consideration that affected our entire tree planting program. Should priority be given to conifers or hardwoods? My preference for hardwood reforestation caused a problem in procuring sufficient planting stock. During the first spring, a McMinnville, Tennessee, nursery shipped tulip poplar. However, due to the earlier growing season in that state, the plants were breaking buds when received.

Project Nursery

A decision was made to grow some of our own planting stock. Consequently, we selected a field for this purpose near the office. Seedbeds, four-feet wide and fifty-feet long, produced a variety of seedlings. In the fall of 1936 through 1939, our own crews gathered seeds. Tulip poplar, white, green, and Biltmore ashes, white, red, and black oaks, and black walnut were immediately planted in the fall. During the ensuing springs, we purchased black locust and sweet gum seeds, which were also planted in order to have a good combination of hardwoods. Nursery laborers removed weeds and did other necessary work. Fortunately, summer rains provided sufficient moisture in the absence of a sprinkling system. No seedlings were planted in the fall, but during the winter tulip poplar and sweet gum suffered from nibbling by cottontail rabbits. Cliff Boling, the local game warden, furnished box traps, and many of these animals found homes elsewhere.

Our nursery continued to produce hardwood seedlings until 1940. Black locust had always been available from the state along with our own supply. We also continued to purchase pines in order to have an adequate supply for employment of the work force.

Hardwood Plantations

Areas on ridge tops and upper slopes were planted with white and black oaks. White and red oaks were mixed with other hardwoods on moist sites at lower elevations. The general rule for locations with better soils and cooler exposures involved combinations of tulip poplar, ashes, white and red oaks, and black walnut. An early experiment in Michigan gave hopes that black walnut growth could be stimulated by planting adjoining rows of black locust. We tried this in a few mixes with other hardwoods. With the exception of one or two rows of black walnut planted along stream banks and old fencerows, it did not exceed 25 percent in mixtures. Sweet gum was added on some bottomland sites. Most combinations included tulip poplar and the oaks. All of these variations offered an opportunity to conduct future research on survival and dominance of each species.

In summary, when the project closed on June 30, 1940, more than 4,000 acres of eroded and cleared land had been planted with forest trees, in addition to those used in wildlife plots. Black locust seedlings on eroded tracts ranked first in the number planted; the availability of conifers meant they ranked second. Hardwoods were last. This planting program required over five million trees

Obliteration of Fences

Various types of fences marked boundaries of properties and field lines. Fences varied from woven wire to a few strands of barbed wire and an occasional rail fence. Some had to remain between purchased and un-optioned farms, but around 300 miles of fences were removed. Timber stand improvement crews removed many while they were working in woodlots. However, it was necessary to assign one crew to this job in open fields. This required the removal of wire and posts. In existing woods, woven wire and barbed wire presented a more difficult task when embedded in desirable trees. Much of the wire was chopped out, but protruding sections were left on each side of the tree when too deeply imbedded. Such fence-row trees are the bane of sawmill operators.

Some fences, of course, marked the exterior boundaries of the project area. Where none existed, surveyors marked the lines. Posts of oak, sassafras, and mulberry with top diameters around seven inches and sloped to face private properties provided adequate identification. The American chestnut, a common tree across the entire southern part of south-central Indiana, would have been used for posts, however, it was rare in the project area. Deam's revision of *Trees of Indiana* reported that the chestnut bark disease (chestnut blight) stretched across the United States by 1934. Evidently, this disease spread rapidly because many trees were dead and being cut by 1935. Sprouts and small trees still persisted in its range after being killed by the disease.

Forest Fire Control

The importance of fire pre-suppression and suppression measures for forests was evident from the outset. Workers were cautioned about forest fires. Employees living within or adjacent to purchase boundaries received special attention. Key personnel were given instructions.

Pre-suppression organization was very important. Fire fighting equipment included a large tank for water transportation placed on a truck during fire seasons. The truck also carried fire pumps (five-gallon size), axes, shovels, brush hooks, fire rakes, torches for back-firing in wooded areas, and rectangular belt beaters attached to long handles for use on field fires. Where ridges had previously been cleared for crops or pastures, a network of ten miles of fire lanes was constructed by use of a

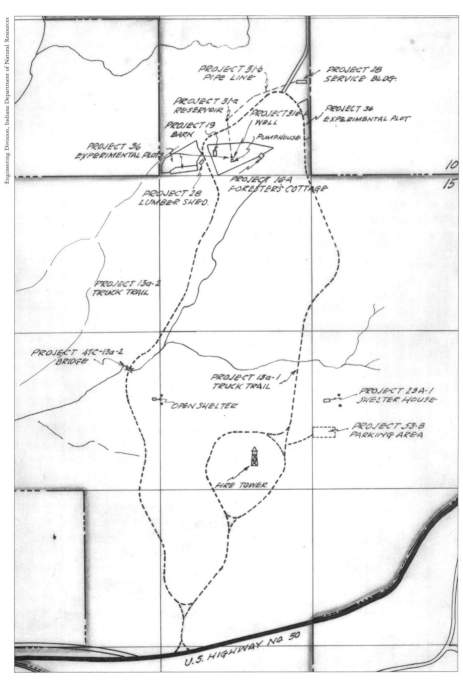

PROJECT 31-b PIPE LINE

PROJECT 28 SERVICE BLDG.

PROJECT 31-a RESERVOIR

PROJECT 31b WELL

PROJECT 36 EXPERIMENTAL PLOT

PROJECT 19 BARN

PUMPHOUSE

PROJECT 36 EXPERIMENTAL PLOTS

PROJECT 16-A FORESTER'S COTTAGE

PROJECT 28 LUMBER SHED.

PROJECT 13a-2 TRUCK TRAIL

PROJECT 47C-13a-2 BRIDGE

PROJECT 13a-1 TRUCK TRAIL

PROJECT 23A-1 SHELTER HOUSE

OPEN SHELTER

PROJECT 53-B PARKING AREA

FIRE TOWER.

U.S. HIGHWAY NO. 50

10

15

Detail of the Martin County State Forest Map prepared by the Indiana Department of
Conservation December 18, 1934. Size of original map 36" x 24"

road grader. These roads also functioned for other activities. Some adjoining water holes served as a source of water for fire suppression.

A high elevation site existed for a fire tower location about one-half mile from our headquarters office. The problem of land acquisition arose again. Ray Kroodsma and I finally talked Everett Inman, who owned the property, into selling enough land for

Outdoor Indiana, April 1934, p. 14

One of the observation towers maintained by the state to aid in the prevention of forest fires. *Outdoor Indiana*, April 1934, p. 14.

the structure and a road to access State Highway 45. Our engineers erected a 100-foot steel fire tower. It was manned during the fall and spring fire seasons. On a clear day, one could see the smokestacks of the Edwardsport hydroelectric plant in Knox County to the west. The fire tower to the southeast in Martin County State Forest and one to the northeast at Little Cincinnati could be tied in by triangulation. Each tower had a round turntable calibrated by 360 degrees. Azimuth readings taken on smoke visible from two or more towers were coordinated to pinpoint the location of the fire, and suppression crews were sent to the site.

During the five-year period of the project there were several fires. The largest one started on the afternoon of March 31, 1940. (On March 28 a small nearby fire pointed to the work of an arsonist.) The large fire of approximately 600 acres started near Ward's Chapel. A stiff west wind blew it toward Indian Springs. A CCC fire fighting crew from the camp at Worthington, Indiana, assisted state and project personnel in finally extinguishing it above the village and railroad tunnel. An Indiana State Police detective and I questioned a suspect living near the site, but we could not obtain a confession.

In the early 1930s, when I worked for the Florida Forest Service, people allowed cattle and razorback hogs to graze or root on any property that was not fenced. A person who killed or ran over livestock on a public highway was liable. Livestock ranged over open areas created by decades of burning the landscape. Piney woods cattle, whose owners did not feed them, were skin and bones by spring if the new tender grass resulting from burning was not available. When wiregrass was not burned each year, it lost much of its palatability. Livestock owners, thus, had an impetus to set fires. This certainly created a frustrating job for a young forester having to manage more than 100 fires in three seasons. Fortunately, new laws and the pulp industry changed the situation by creating a market for growing pines on a short rotation. Improved pastures also replaced wiregrass where several acres were once necessary to sustain one cow. Controlled burning is now practiced on some areas not being used by the pulp industry.

Water Holes

A shortage of water existed in many parts of the project area. It was necessary to create water holes and small ponds as an emergency supply for fire fighting. It also helped create a much better distribution of wildlife. The first impoundment near the West Union road required the rental of horses with drivers for pulling slip scoops to excavate fill material for this pond. A small tractor with a front blade soon replaced the horse-drawn equipment, and a total of 141 small water holes, primarily for wildlife, served a beneficial purpose for fire control. Few of the ponds had sufficient depths to be stocked with fish. This plan was soon discarded in favor of small excavations on flatter land with gentle slopes. The upland Zanesville soils only required a watershed ratio of two or three to one due to a hardpan in the subsoil. Grass overflow waterways gave adequate protection. A few water holes located on steeper slopes washed out or were filled with sediment in a few months. The value of these water holes to wildlife could be attested by countless tracks of birds and mammals. One of the larger ponds stocked with fish is now known as Lost Lake. Beaver have assisted by building a higher dam.

Nature Center

Natural history features associated with the present and future management of the area as a state forest were displayed in an unoccupied building at the work camp. The papier-mâché relief map used at the Graham Farm Fair in Daviess County depicted the lake, roads, foot trails, buildings, public use area, and green forest cover after conversion to state ownership. Dried specimens of indigenous tree and shrub leaves were mounted on large display sheets containing identification information. Workers hauled stump sections, cut during the removal of the last old-growth stand remaining on the Judge Dillon tract on the Portersville Road in Dubois County, to the center. These stumps included white oak, black oak, black walnut, and tulip poplar. Some were 300 years old, and different chronological dates in the history of the United States, before and after European settlement, were marked at appropriate annual rings.

Luther Corbin, a worker who had taken a correspondence course in taxidermy, mounted specimens of reptiles, birds, and mammals. I had a collector's permit for taking protected and unprotected animals. Most of those on display were unprotected or taken during open hunting seasons. Although the goshawk was not protected, I regretted shooting a beautiful specimen; it was an uncommon winter visitor to Indiana. The reptiles included a 53-inch timber rattler.

The entire exhibit attracted many persons and represented another example of public relations. I do not know about the subsequent disposal of the specimens, but assume that they were lost. Present-day regulations monitored by authorized agencies require strict rules for the preservation of birds and mammals on display or in collections.

Outdoor Indiana, April 1934, p. 14

(Left to Right) William Seng, Sr., William Seng, Jr., Ray Mathies, and Edward Seng stand under a large black oak on the Dillon Tract in Dubois County.

Arboretum

In addition to a nature center, another tract with living trees and shrubs was established east of the public use area. This arboretum featured local native species as well as those collected from other parts of Indiana. It was patterned after the one made by Dr. Charles Deam at his home in Bluffton, Indiana. It had been my good fortune to accompany him on several field trips during the summer of 1935, my last CCC assignment before coming to Martin County. He was getting older and was happy to have me drive his car and carry plant presses. We traveled to many locations around the state.

I used the same system of quadrants and marked each corner with discarded limestone slabs obtained from a Bedford quarry. The location of each tree or shrub was recorded on three-inch by five-inch cards. Deam had used zinc markers and gave me the formula for a solution that would etch into them. One dram of copper chloride was mixed in one ounce of water. Zinc sheets were cut into rectangular markers and fastened to number nine galvanized wire for insertion into the ground. The common and scientific name, range, and other information could still be read fifty years later.

This rustic sign marked the beginning of the foot trail on the south side of Lake Greenwood.

Foot Trails

A foot trail on the south side of Lake Greenwood provided an opportunity for hikers and nature lovers to enjoy the scenic beauty of the area. It began near the junction of State Highway 45 and the road leading to the public use area. A large rustic sign with an overhanging roof stood at the beginning of the trail. It contained a map in back of a glass enclosure and showed the outline of the trail and other pertinent information. Construction criteria for the work crew included a four-foot-wide path with grades not to exceed 20 percent and footbridges where necessary.

Directional markers depicted the outline of a footprint burned into a small tulip poplar board. These were attached to low posts along the trail. The trail led downhill past the arboretum and around the picnic area to the end of the embayment where boats were to be launched. From there, it skirted the shoreline across from the boathouse and proceeded near the water through woods and fields with open vistas of Lake Greenwood. The trail then led uphill through a large field with a view of Little Creek on the opposite side of the lake. Then, it continued at a higher elevation around some valleys and ended at the dam.

Another short foot trail began at the boathouse and followed the south bank of the lake to its upper end.

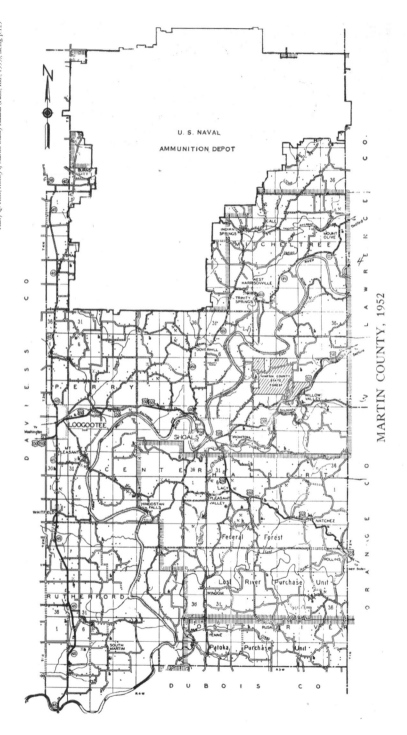

Harry Q. Holt, *History of Martin County Indiana* (Paoli, Ind., 1953), facing p.125

MARTIN COUNTY, 1952

THE MANAGEMENT OF FISH AND WILDLIFE RESOURCES

The Division of Fish and Game showed great interest in the fish and wildlife resources in the project area of Martin County. In fact, during the development period, Kenneth M. Kunkle, director of the Division of Fish and Game, Henry P. Cottingham, superintendent of game, John Gotschalk, superintendent of fisheries, John Roll, chief game warden, and V. M. Simmons, commissioner of the Indiana Department of Conservation, all inspected the operations of this project. The project priority was stocking Lake Greenwood and planting aquatic vegetation. The establishment of wildlife refuges created much interest, as did the release of pen-raised wild turkeys. Officials requested reports on experimental releases of chukar partridges and California Valley quail. Brooding pens for raising bobwhite quail were constructed for future use. Management of wildlife, in particular, was in its infancy, and many practices went through great changes in later years.

The Division of Fish and Game selected the new work camp as the site for a two-week training course for game wardens. C. R. Gutermuth headed the educational section of the agency, and he prepared a large mimeographed training manual. Students were housed and fed by camp personnel; a barracks provided ample space for a classroom. Classes were conducted in law enforcement, administrative policy, public relations, and current fish and wildlife management practices.

Fish Resources

At that time, the Division of Fish and Game managed the state's fish hatcheries for fish stocking purposes. Game wardens enforced laws regarding length and possession limits of game species and the closed period during their spawning season from May 1 to June 15. Along with other activities, wardens searched for illegal nets, traps, and other devices. Both the Division of Fish and Game and the Division of Forestry participated during the Lake Greenwood development period. Fishing was of minor importance before construction of the dam. There were spring runs of suckers, as well as some indigenous game and nongame fishes in the streams in the area.

The dam for Lake Greenwood was completed in late 1937. After the de-watering conduit near the base of this impoundment was closed, the lake started to slowly fill. However, the Avoca State Fish Hatchery in Lawerence County began delivering fish while the dam was under construction. A temporary impoundment, using long logs removed from an old cabin, was placed across Furse Creek at an upstream location. Stocking included parent largemouth, smallmouth, and rock bass along with bluegills. Unfortunately, a heavy rain overflowed the banks and caused the dam to wash out. This permitted the fish to escape downstream. Stocking in 1938, involving parent fish released before the spawning season, included 1,100 largemouth bass, 2,500 smallmouth bass, 2,200 rock bass, 1,250 crappies, 2,000 redear sunfish, and 63,200 bluegills.

In the summer of 1938, our crews used a flatbed truck and metal horse tank with a pump for aeration to transport fish stranded in river cutoffs near Elnora, Indiana. A seine, drawn across these temporary pools in the West Fork of White River, yielded several thousand bass, crappie, channel catfish, bullheads, and a wide variety of different species of sunfishes. Workers returned all minnows and rough fish to the river. However, there had also been the annual spring run of suckers in Furse Creek, and these and other indigenous species remained after impoundment. Reported numbers for 1939 were 4,000 largemouth and 1,350 smallmouth bass, 118 crappies, and 71,000 bluegills. The 1940 stocking included 26,000 smallmouth, 8,600 largemouth, and 1,000 rock bass along with 18,500 redear sunfish, 1,000 crappies, and 3,150 bullheads.

Two fish rearing ponds, with more than one acre of surface water, were built below the dam. Water was piped from the north side of the lake. Largemouth bass fry, delivered in June 1938, grew to a suitable size by fall. In addition to soybean

HATCHERIES and REARING PONDS

for

BASS and SUNFISH

By A. E. ANDREWS
Superintendent of Fish Hatcheries

———

1935

———

DIVISION OF FISH AND GAME
DEPARTMENT OF CONSERVATION
INDIANA

The Division of Fish and Game issued instructional manuals to aid in the proper construction and maintenance of rearing ponds.

meal for feeding, piles of cow manure were placed along the sodded banks. Workers gradually pushed the manure into the water in order to produce zooplankton-like daphne and other minute animal life for young fish to feed upon. The bass were released into the lake when cannibalism became evident.

The Division of Fish and Game contracted with an aquatic nursery in Wisconsin to plant vegetative cover in the lake. This included wild celery, wapeto duck potato, coontail moss, burreed, water lily, and pondweed. These were commercial names for a number of different species. For example, burreeds belong to the Sparganiaceae family which comprises several species. Coontail moss is a hornwort widely scattered over the state. The purchase of these plants was of little value. Wild celery does not grow in this kind of an impoundment in Indiana. Waterfowl and other birds bring in seeds of coontail moss and different pondweeds that become established and maintain their own dominances. In fact, many species could cause problems by creating dense beds of aquatic vegetation.

The lake was not opened for fishing until June 16, 1940. Unfortunately, a serious leak in the dam made it necessary to drain the impoundment in the early spring before the fishing season even opened. Thus, most of the prior fish stockings were lost. However, many fish remained in the old stream channel below the bottom of the de-watering conduit. Traps placed in the channel below this dam captured some escaping fish. Seining crews also aided in this effort. All fish were transported and released in Lake Lenape in Shakamak State Park. After the deposit of a thick layer of clay on the upstream side of the leaking part of the dam, impoundment of water began again on November 8, 1940. The lake did not become completely full until 1942.

When comparing the present management of fishery resources with that in the 1930s, it is evident that many changes have taken place. In an impoundment like Lake Greenwood, smallmouth and rock bass should not have been used. The high numbers of bluegills caused early stunting as well as their consumption of small bass fry. Redear sunfish with lower reproduction would not have resulted in this early over population. Stocking fish that were seined out of the river was wrong, as were later releases of northern pike.

Another experimental fish release not connected with Lake Greenwood took place in the summer of 1937. The Division of Fish and Game had been stocking some cold-water streams in northern Indiana with brook, rainbow, and brown trout. As reproduction was nil, trout fishermen simply caught them after each release in the spring with little carryover in subsequent years. Temperatures of the water flowing from the spring near Sargent's Store in McCameron Township averaged around 56 degrees Fahrenheit. So, the division delivered 1,260 fingerling rainbow trout for experimental releases. Turkey Creek below Sargent's Store was shaded on each side and received one-half of these fish. The remainder was liberated in the pool where the cold water emerged from a spring at Mountain Springs in Baker Township. Its tributary stream flowed into Sulphur Creek. The volume of cold water flowing from each source was insufficient and despite the tree cover along both release streams, their temperatures reached 80 degrees Fahrenheit a few hundred yards downstream. These streams were too warm for trout. A small number remained for a short time in the mouth of the spring at Mountain Springs, and they would dart out when bread was thrown into the water.

A personal event that concerned another inhabitant of the streams occurred in the summer of 1939. Bill Seng, along with his brother Ed and neighbor Ted Heeke from Dubois County, took me on a turtle hunt. A section of Indian Creek, east of Mountain Springs and across the line in Lawrence County, was selected for this purpose. Since I was a neophyte, they gave me a sack as we waded downstream. I certainly did not object, but I had my doubts about the whole affair of catching snapping turtles with bare hands. Ted appeared to be the most experienced so I followed him. At a bend in the stream, a drift of branches had lodged against the bank. He stuck his arm into the drift and started to feel around. Out came his arm and hand holding a squirming snapping turtle by its tail. This action involved the placement of one hand on the top of the carapace and slowly moving the other hand around the side to the serrated notches above the tail. The party kept me busy wading back and forth in the stream. The turtles were dumped out of a sack into the car trunk. We must have captured at least a dozen nice ones that Saturday morning. I immediately butchered them in anticipation of delicious fried turtle and soup. Turtle soup has always been a favorite item in the Dubois County restaurants.

It should also be mentioned that the population of bullfrogs greatly increased during this same period at Lake Greenwood. My brother-in-law, Chet Clements, and I borrowed a boat for catching them one night in July. One of us paddled the boat while the other searched the shoreline with a strong flashlight. The frog's eyes illuminated in the bright beam as the boat was maneuvered close enough to capture it with one hand. We caught around twenty-five, and some still croaked after being placed in sacks. In these ways, we enhanced our summer menus with fish from Hindostan Falls, turtle meat, and frog legs.

Wildlife Resources

The Division of Fish and Game also managed the wildlife resources. It placed great emphasis on the artificial propagation of bobwhite quail and ring-necked pheasants. Two large game farms raised adults for their eggs. When the chicks hatched, the farms delivered the one-day-old chicks to conservation clubs. Unsuccessful attempts were also made with Hungarian partridges, ruffed grouse, and prairie chickens. Large refuge areas were maintained for protection of game species. Game wardens also enforced bag and possession limits on all game species along with laws regarding certain furbearing animals. Protective measures received their major attention, along with the popular release programs. The division did not conduct any wildlife research. However, it requested our cooperation in collecting information about some experimental releases. All of these activities are explained in order to describe the management of wildlife on the project under these existing policies.

Wildlife Refuges

Federal and state agencies recommended the establishment of large wildlife refuges. Indiana did not have a federal refuge. However, all land owned by the Department of Conservation was closed to hunting. The Division of Fish and Game maintained large areas of several thousand acres on the Jasper-Pulaski State Game Preserve in the two counties and the Kankakee State Game Preserve in Starke County. Another small area was on the Wells County State Forest and Game Preserve. A large tract had also been acquired with hunting and fishing license funds in Brown County, but it became Brown County State Park. In fact, all of the fish and game properties were closed to hunting until the early 1940s when sportsmen's money was used for buying state fish and game areas (now state fish and wildlife areas). The Hovey Lake property in Posey County was the first to allow hunting.

The Division of Forestry did not permit hunting, citing prevention of forest fires as the reason. During World War II, T. E. Shaw, Purdue University Extension Forester, as acting state forester, agreed to permit this sport on an experimental basis in 1944 with the provision that a resulting forest fire would cause closure. The Division of Fish and Game placed signs and a box with information warning about forest fires at main entrance roads where hunters obtained hunting cards for recording successes. No forest fires occurred. In 1945, the division furnished metal boundary signs for all properties. A strand of wire also surrounded buildings and picnic grounds to prohibit hunting at those public locations. The Martin County project had 3,740 acres in refuges. The largest refuge surrounded the former Dwyer property where turkeys were released. If restocking efforts had been successful, this large refuge would have been justified, especially if it had included initial releases of deer. However, existing small upland game like bobwhite quail, cottontail rabbits, and squirrels had range requirements limited to only a few acres of suitable habitats. There was no justification for the closure of the earlier large-game preserves.

One work crew was assigned the duty of placing one strand of number-nine wire around refuge boundaries. Crews had already been instructed to staple wires to unmerchantable trees. In cases where none were present, merchantable trees were used and protected with a short piece of two-by-four nailed to the tree. This permitted the wire to be pushed out as the tree grew. The same method functioned for metal refuge signs placed at two-rod intervals.

Food and Cover Plots

Planting trees, shrubs, and annuals for wildlife food and cover improved the carrying capacity for small game species in open fields, especially during emergency periods in late winter. The center of each plot had rows of different trees and shrubs of value to both game and nongame birds and mammals. During the five-year period, a total of 20,000 Russian olive, crabapple, and various species of dogwoods and viburnums provided permanent cover as well as seasonal food.

Annual strips on both sides of them contained sunflower, milo, Sudan grass, cowpeas, and other experimental plants in order to determine preferences by various kinds of wildlife. Goldfinches, cardinals, and other songbirds stripped sunflower seed heads in the early fall. In later years, biologists found that the seed became an important September food for mourning doves. Wheatland milo had seed stalks remaining above snow, which bobwhites sometimes ate. Their tracks could be noted in the snow. However, they did not use it to any great extent. Black amber sorghum later proved to be more valuable, as attested by the purple color of bobwhite droppings in overnight roosts. Sudan grass and cowpeas did not prove to be of importance.

Rabbits nibbled on different plants and damaged some of the trees and shrubs by debarking them. Workers planted annuals each year. The plots averaged one acre in size and were scattered in 325 patches. One hunter obtained a map showing their locations, then drove along the roads and turned his two pointer dogs loose on nearby plots. If they pointed, he would flush the covey and then drive to the next patch. I should have been more cautious in hiding the maps from this type of hunter.

This experiment with wildlife plantings aided in determining the size and composition of plants to be used in establishing wildlife habitats. The Division of Fish and Game later adopted this practice under its Pittman-Robertson Wildlife Habitat Restoration Project 6D. Private landowners signed ten year leases to set aside two-to-ten-acre tracts as refuges for wildlife. Each annual planting did not need to be as large as our experimental ones, and this size of a refuge area was large enough for small game.

Game Management

The transition from private to public ownership of the project land dictated the initiation of future wildlife management in favor of the white-tailed deer, wild turkey, and ruffed grouse. The production of timber on a sustained yield basis in a state forest remained the most important priority. However, good game management practices were implemented as an important integral feature of the overall plan. This prompted a biological survey of existing wildlife populations and habitat conditions in order to formulate plans for this future transition.

Some compromises between management of timber and game took place. In conjunction with timber stand improvement, a fifty-foot-wide strip around the edges of woodlands was left in its natural state. The vines of wild grape, woodbine, bittersweet, and poison ivy remained along with all trees and shrubs, many of which had value for wildlife. At that time, the dense underbrush offered escape and nesting cover for bobwhites and nongame birds. These values would continue to function for woodland species for many future years. From a forestry standpoint, these strips also reduced the drying effects of winds blowing in from open spaces.

When timber stand improvement took place, brush piles and wildlife shelters were built on the edge. Four stakes with forks on top were driven into the ground. Two cross poles held brush placed across them. The four sides beneath were left open to discourage predation. Otherwise, this could become a problem if they were used as regular feeding stations during the winter. They were of primary utility as emergency sites where corn could be placed during severe weather.

We modified interior timber stand work by leaving one den tree per acre. Girdling of other large den trees, instead of felling them, permitted wolf trees, especially beech, to gradually die and lose their branches over a long period of time. The resulting opening beneath them permitted the invasion of a diversity of young trees and other vegetation. If a merchantable tree had a visible den, this also sufficed for this modification.

Release Studies

The popularity of artificial propagation of bobwhite quail and ring-necked pheasants continued for many years. This program entailed major expenditures by the Division of Fish and Game without any effort to examine its validity. An interest arose concerning the use of California Valley quail and chukar partridges. This time, however, we received a request to make releases and submit a report on our findings.

On March 31, 1938, the Wells County Game Farm delivered seventeen adult California Valley quail. The farm had raised these birds from a shipment of eggs received the previous year. These beautiful birds with a curved plume were released at two locations. Six were liberated near the lake bottom and eleven were released in an orchard near the home built for the forest superintendent. The holding boxes were placed on the ground, and the releases were observed from a distance in order to not frighten the birds. After leaving the opened side doors on the boxes, some emerged and pecked around in the grass, while others flew into trees. Workers and persons living in the area were requested to report sightings.

We made no further observations of the small release near the lake bottom, but the quail in the larger covey on the upland proved more interesting. Liberation in the early spring permitted pairing and nesting possibilities. There were no reports during that summer, but sightings of two adults began on December 8, 1938, near the original release site. The two quail were feeding on corn at the horse barn near the forest superintendent's house. Three additional observations of these two males were made between that time and January 3, 1939. In March, Mrs. L. C. Pickett, who lived in the house at that time, reported one in a covey of native bobwhites feeding nearby.

In April, two companions and I observed one California Valley quail and one bobwhite hen crossing the road near the above location. Likewise, a mixed pair was noted near there in May. It was noteworthy that two different species of quail congregated together. The weather was mild during that winter, but the several observations of two imported birds remaining alone was quite unusual. No nests were ever found, nor any evidence of adults with young. A few adults did join with a bobwhite covey before pairing off. No reports were received about any being bagged during the two fall hunting seasons.

Fifty chukar partridges were also delivered concurrently with the imported quail. Five groups of eight and one of ten were released using the method described above. Some immediately flew in various directions. Release sites in McCameron Township were located where ridge tops and side slopes contained more open fields. Many of the chukars just seemed to disappear in a short period after a few reported sightings. Two negative reports were submitted to the Division of Fish and Game. The beautiful multicolored quail were subjected to an environment much different than their West Coast habitat. Likewise, the chukar partridges found the hills of Martin County quite different from their native dry rocky region in Asia.

I did not hear of any subsequent releases of the nonnative quail. Propagation and releases of chukars continued for some years. The Martin County study, of course, had been conducted with too few birds and lacked a biological investigation by trained personnel. After the Pittman-Robertson Wildlife Research Project 2R began in 1940, representative areas in different regions of the state were used for detailed observations. Final conclusions stated the unsuitability of these partridges as a game bird in Indiana. This experiment saved the state future high expenditures of funds.

This was in contrast with expensive releases of the ring-necked pheasant. Over a period of many years, they were liberated in all parts of the state without an investigation of their suitability, and now persist in numbers only in the north-western prairie section of Indiana. The Burns City Conservation Club raised these birds in 1937 and released them on the Asbury Holt farm and other locations. Very few were seen or shot during the first hunting season for pheasants that opened in November of that year. The Odon Conservation Club also raised them for several years, with best recoveries in the former wet prairie west of that town. The project area, like the rest of the state originally covered with forests, was not a suitable habitat.

Bobwhite Quail

The native bobwhite quail has always been the favorite game bird of sportsmen and farmers. Clearing of the original forest resulted in its statewide distribution, with higher population in southern Indiana which has milder temperatures. Small fields with crops, fencerows, and adjoining edges of woody cover provided an ideal habitat. The purchases of farms by the federal government eliminated cropland, but created a temporary favorable environment for the quail.

This temporary transition caused a change in the food habits of quail. With blocks of land no longer planted in corn and other farm crops, ragweed, foxtail, and smartweed became abundant on fallow farm fields. These weed seeds were important fall foods. Korean lespedeza, used for erosion control, also provided a good substitute for corn. I often found quail with crops full of this seed during the hunting season. However, the most critical period for survival of quail and other wildlife occurred in the winter. During the cold winter of 1939–1940, snow lay on the ground for several weeks, and natural and planted foods were not available. In spots where it was not too deep, quail would actually scratch through the snow in search of Korean lespedeza seeds and native foods. Corn was also distributed to local employees for emergency feeding.

Increases in food and cover caused bobwhite populations on the project area to increase and attract hunters. Officials from the Indianapolis office of the Division of Fish and Game hunted here. Lawrence Bauer, a Loogootee bird hunter, even started a guide service. Local hunters, in addition to gaining permission to use farms in other parts of the county, also used the open project area. Max Sargent, who delivered mail on a route out of Burns City, knew about the locations of many coveys. The daily limit was ten birds during the forty-day open season. Some hunters took vacations; others hunted on holidays and Saturdays. Hunting was closed on Sundays. It was not unusual for some of the better shooters to bag from 100 to 150 quail during the season. Martin County quail hunters averaged twenty-two per season. Hunters also bagged an occasional woodcock during their migration and before freezing weather when they could no longer probe with their long bills in search of food in the soft earth.

There was obviously little need to stock pen-raised birds, but local conservation clubs released surviving numbers of their 350-day-old chicks. Future studies conducted by Pittman-Robertson Wildlife Research Project 2R found that bobwhites released at eight weeks of age in the summer were of no significant importance.

After the banding of several thousand, only 6 percent of the bands were recovered by hunters.

Ruffed Grouse and Prairie Chicken

Different species of birds prefer different habitats. Ruffed grouse were originally abundant in Martin County. They preferred woodlands and bordering cover and probably reached peak populations during the early clearing of the land, which resulted in more forest edges. However, unlike the bobwhite, their numbers began to decline with the decrease in forested acreages. They are gallinaceous birds, the same as greater prairie chickens, which, in contrast, preferred open wet and dry grasslands.

It is of interest that the greater prairie chicken inhabited such areas in adjoining Greene and Daviess counties. A farmer, who lived next to a former wet prairie west of Odon, told me that prairie chickens did not disappear until 1932 on his farm, which bordered this earlier drained wetland. An occasional prairie chicken may have wandered into the western edge of Martin County.

The ruffed grouse was abundant in most parts of the state before Anglo-American settlement; at that time 87 percent of the land in pre-settlement Indiana was forest and only 13 percent prairie. By the late 1930s, the ruffed grouse was primarily confined to the Norman Upland with scattered remnants in the southern part of the Crawford Upland. R. E. Mumford recorded a last report for this bird in Martin County in 1934. Lilbern Ellis, who lived in the resettlement area, reported their disappearance from his farm in 1928. No reports were received between 1935 and 1940, and none were seen during the biological survey. Hunting seasons for ruffed grouse and prairie chickens were closed in 1937.

Waterfowl

Lake Greenwood primarily functioned as a resting place for migrating ducks and geese during the fall and spring. When the lake was filling, a few Canada geese stopped, as well as dabbling ducks, like mallards. Waterfowl populations increased as the surface area enlarged. Fourteen wood duck nesting boxes were erected in summer 1938, when there were some resident wood ducks along with pied-billed grebes. These were joined in early September by migrating blue-winged teal and later by coots. A few Canada geese and some mallards arrived in October, but the southward movement of larger flocks did not occur until freezing weather in the north in late November and early December 1938.

The lake soon became alive with honks and quacks. Mallards, wood ducks, and black ducks, in descending order of abundance, were the major species, followed by pintails, widgeons, and green-winged teal. All of these dabbling ducks and coots were scattered on the lake along with a few diving ducks. The dabbling ducks and geese only fed by dipping in shallow water. As there was a shortage of such areas, it was necessary for them to either leave after a few days or fly to other feeding places. A few Canada geese made daily flights to the vicinity of the confluence of Haw Creek with the East Fork of White River. The others, along with ducks, fed in the closer cornfields in Greene County and the West Fork of White River. The onset of cold weather signaled their general exodus to southern wintering locations.

The spring migration varied with more diving ducks using the lake. Indiana is situated on the eastern portion of the Mississippi Flyway. Most fall flights of scaup, ring-necked ducks, redheads, and canvasbacks, especially those that flew to the Atlantic Flyway, missed Indiana. In the spring, lesser scaup appeared in numbers, and many ring-necks sometimes remained until early May before leaving for northern breeding grounds. Waterfowl hunting had not been an important sport in this county. I do not know of anyone who hunted on Lake Greenwood during this period.

Other Birds

Lake Greenwood also attracted other species associated with water. In August 1938, a flock of at least fifty little blue herons frequented the shallow end of the lake. These immature birds, with their juvenile white plumage, waded and fed along the edges. They had wandered north from their southern nesting grounds. During the same period, a small flock of ten or fifteen great egrets used the same places. The appearance of little blue herons was of interest in 1938; thousands had been reported in Indiana in 1930. Kingfishers found this new fishing area, as did green herons. Solitary great blue herons also waded along the shorelines.

A walk along the foot trail on the south side of the lake provided evidence of biodiversity and ornithology in the area. Summer inhabitants of forests and fields provided pleasurable observations for studies of the distribution of birds in different environments. One could take the trail where it entered the woods on the west side of the embankment across from the marina and listen to the constant calls of the red-eyed vireo, the high lisping notes of the blue-gray gnatcatcher, and the plaintive song of the wood pewee. Acadian flycatchers and great crested flycatchers flitted around in the high branches. Other common birds in the trees were the wood thrush, scarlet tanager, blue jay, tufted titmouse, and white-breasted nuthatch. Cerulean warblers and some redstarts further contributed to the colorful bird life in the canopy. Flickers and downy and red-bellied woodpeckers made their presence known, along with an occasional red-headed woodpecker. Pileated woodpeckers were rare due to the absence of older mature stands.

Ground cover, young trees, and shrubs on the forest floor attracted birds to nest and feed there. Ovenbirds, with their teacher calls, were common among the mayapple and fern beds. Kentucky warblers and worm-eating warblers also used this favorable cover. Brown-headed cowbirds searched for nests where they could lay their eggs. In forested areas as well as other habitats, they favored the nests of small birds like warblers and sparrows. After removing an egg from the nest, the female cowbird would deposit her egg for the foster parent to incubate and raise.

In some locations, the trail emerged into sites that were reverting from open fields or pastures into areas with various stages of forbs, briars, shrubs, and sapling trees. This biota of flora and fauna created a different ecosystem from the forest. It was further augmented by the edge effect where woods and more open conditions provided a better diversity in the environment. The combination of various cover types resulted in a higher carrying capacity for birds and mammals when compared with large forested tracts. Woodland edges attracted cardinals, gray catbirds, and Carolina chickadees. Indigo buntings joined the inhabitants of the more open areas. Saplings provided perches where yellow-breasted chats, indigo buntings, rufous-sided towhees, song sparrows, and other singing males established their territorial rights against other invading males. Prairie warblers preferred habitat on more eroded sites.

The trail also passed through pastures and hay fields that had been maintained by farmers prior to acquisition. These grasslands did not support as many different types of birds. However, the field sparrow was very common. Grass-hopper and vesper sparrows and dickcissels also joined the cacophony of songs along with the eastern meadowlark. Kestrels often hovered in the air above these places. These little falcons with rapid wing beats were able to remain in a stationary position while they searched for mice and insects in the grass. These open spaces provided views of turkey vultures soaring in the thermals. Eastern kingbirds often chased crows. They, in turn, would take out their frustrations by harassing owls and red-tailed hawks in adjacent woods. In places where these grasslands adjoined previously cultivated fields, fencerows provided a more varied habitat. They were favorite spots for robins, song sparrows, mourning doves, eastern kingbirds, and bobwhite quail.

The foot trail approached Lake Greenwood above the place where settlers had once stalked white-tailed deer a century earlier. The lick was now under water. Belted kingfishers had already discovered a new fishing ground, rough-winged swallows and barn swallows flitted over the water in search of insects, and chimney swifts twittered and flew in circles above them. Red-winged blackbirds and common grackles frequented the bordering shoreline, and yellow warblers, common yellowthroats, and other species used adjoining brushy thickets and scattered trees.

After meandering uphill in order to skirt above coves, the trail descended and ended at the dam. It passed a recently vacated farmstead with standing buildings. In the small barn, barn swallows fed their young in mud-plastered nests attached to floor beams over the horse stalls. House sparrows had untidy, bulky nests of

After its construction, the 800-acre Lake Greenwood became a much needed resting place for migrating waterfowl, pictured here in the shallow end of the lake.

grass, straw, and any other available material. In the yard there was a large elm where a northern oriole flew back and forth to its hanging nest. A house wren sang in a nearby grape arbor, and a chipping sparrow on the lawn continued its rapid buzzing song. Other birds were the robin, cardinal, and mourning dove. The many different habitats along this trail brought about the diversity of bird-life found over the project area.

Wild Turkey

Wild turkey hunting season in Indiana was closed in 1903. The turkey had once been a common game bird in the area. Mr. Porter, who lived in McCameron Township and was eighty-five years old when I interviewed him, had shot at least fifty turkeys during his lifetime. He recalled seeing the last one on the Fred Toon place about two miles east of Burns City. He could not recall the date.

The Division of Fish and Game became interested in reintroducing this large game bird after it obtained some eggs from the state of Pennsylvania. Wild tom turkeys could fly into fenced enclosures there and mate with wing-clipped hens. The Division of Fish and Game incubated the eggs and delivered twenty-five turkeys during the summer of 1937. In the meantime, an enclosure with a high fence had been placed in the largest game refuge in the area. The young birds were fed for a short time to become acclimated to the wooded tract adjoining an open field where they could find insects to supplement other foods. However, predation by great-horned owls and red-tailed hawks probably occurred, and the turkeys were immediately turned loose. The last reported sighting was in the ensuing winter. This restoration method proved unsuccessful because the young birds were without wild adults and they were already semidomesticated. Our investigations showed ample food and cover for wild turkeys.

White-Tailed Deer

The hunting season for white-tailed deer closed in 1903. Evidently, their population was low, and the last ones disappeared within a few years. Between 1934 and 1940, small numbers were reintroduced in southern Indiana, but none in Martin County. A farmer reported seeing one in the area in 1934. Six each had been released in Dubois and Orange counties during that year, and this animal probably wandered from one of these counties. William Payton observed two in the summer of 1937. No other reports were received during the entire development era.

Early Hunting Experiences

Northern Martin County must have been a prime habitat in early settlement times. Eph Inman, in his book, *Stories of Hatfield, the Pioneer*, vividly describes Emmanuel Hatfield's experiences in Martin, Green and Lawrence counties after moving from the Cumberland Mountains in Tennessee in 1831. During a period of twelve years, he shot 978 whitetails. From his cabin near Owensburg, he would wander over the hills to Furs Creek, its early name. Deer were plentiful, especially near a lick on the south side of that valley. He and his brother also built a log bear trap on the north slope above this creek and caught one there. When he camped overnight at the Rock House in western McCameron Township, the screams of the catamount (bobcat) echoed from the surrounding forest. The mountain lion or panther, an animal of the wilderness, disappeared at an early date. Bison and elk were also gone.

E. Inman, *Stories of Hatfield, the Pioneer* (2nd ed., New Albany, Ind.: Ledger Co., 1890)

Engraving from Inman's *Stories of Hatfield, the Pioneer*, showing early settlers using dogs for treeing animals.

E. Inman, *Stories of Hatfield, the Pioneer* (2nd ed., New Albany, Ind.: Ledger Co., 1890)

EMMANUEL HATFIELD.

Emmanuel Hatfield, the settler featured in *Stories of Hatfield, the Pioneer,* told of life in Martin, Green, and Lawrence counties in the project era.

Cottontail Rabbit

The small populations of cottontail rabbits in pre-settlement times were due to the same environmental factors that existed for bobwhite quail. The numbers of cottontail rabbits increased with more diverse habitats after settlement. The land purchased in the 1930s for resettlement purposes contained a high carrying capacity for rabbits with its small fields for crops, hay, and pastures surrounded with fencerows. When farming practices were discontinued during development years, the invasion of weeds and other herbaceous cover caused a temporary increase in cottontails. The increase in the cottontail population on the project area caused problems in hardwood plantations and especially in the forest nursery. In winter, rabbit damage became critical as they clipped back the tops of seedlings in the beds.

Gray and Fox Squirrels

Martin County originally supported a vast wilderness with gray and fox squirrels as major components of the small animal population. Gray squirrels were far more abundant than fox squirrels, which preferred more edge cover along streams or places with poor timber stands. The preponderance of forested cover on the area of the project in the 1930s also supported a greater gray squirrel population, as attested by records collected from hunters. The smaller woods, with more edges bordering farmland, no doubt had a higher carrying capacity for fox squirrels. I recall many early morning and late evening hunts for these animals. A few other "nimrods" used rifles with scopes, but the shotgun was preferred for grays in southern Indiana.

Squirrel populations fluctuated from year to year in accordance with mast crops of acorns and hickory nuts, with beechnuts, walnuts, and other foods of secondary importance. A poor mast production curtailed the main breeding season in the winter, and that resulted in lower populations in the ensuing hunting season. However, due to the large wooded areas, it was not as severe as in isolated small woodlots.

In earlier years, the hunting season opened on August 1, but in later years, not until August 15. Both dates occurred before the main hickory nut and acorn crops were ripe. Squirrels would be feeding on tulip poplar, black gum, ironwood, black cherry, and sampling immature hickory nuts. Also, in years when sugar maples were thick with their double-winged seeds, squirrels were always able to choose the one full side and discard the other blind one.

Some controversy existed regarding the early opening of the hunting season, especially as it related to female squirrels. In some years, when there was a poor mast crop, old female squirrels often did not bring off their first litter in the winter. In the second ensuing breeding season in the late spring, both old and younger females had litters. Some were late, resulting in the shooting of pregnant or suckling females.

Squirrel hunting was, and still is, an early season popular pastime in Martin and other counties in southern Indiana. In considering the average resident in the area, it is safe to say that squirrel hunting was their favorite sport. There were the usual boasters like Jim Huff, who would often tell about a shagbark hickory full of squirrels where one could limit out. Some hunters, especially those caught hunting before the season opened, spoke of squirrels having therapeutic values for sick persons.

Red and Gray Foxes

The gray fox, like the gray squirrel, inhabited the vast forests that once covered Martin County. In fact, some question if its red brother was an inhabitant in early times. During resettlement days, red foxes were more widespread and of greater interest. Fox chasers and fox hunters had different thoughts about hunting both species. Fox chasers, who used foxhounds for the pleasure of the chase, were adamant in their opposition to trapping or shooting them. This was especially true for the red fox, which would run longer without escaping into holes as did the gray. These persons in the area followed the hounds or gathered at night around a campfire to try to determine which dog was leading the pack. They would sometimes be unable to find their dogs at the end of the chase, and it was not uncommon to hear the hounds still running the next day. Fox hunters and trappers considered foxes to be destructive because they killed game birds, rabbits, and poultry.

The dried scats of foxes found along game trails showed rabbit fur, mice bones, and persimmon seeds in the fall and winter. In order to gain more information on the food habits of the fox, arrangements were made with the U.S. Bureau of Biological Survey in Washington, D.C., to ship to it stomachs of gray and red foxes for food analysis. Cooperating trappers and hunters were provided with cheesecloth that could be tied into bags for holding the contents. These collections were placed in a formulin solution for shipment. This study was nationwide; no summary of our particular series was ever received. However, a later investigation by the Pittman-

Robertson Wildlife Research Project of the Indiana Division of Fish and Game revealed on a statewide basis the winter diet of red foxes. Eighty-eight percent had rabbit remains; 58 percent mice; 32 percent non-game birds; 20 percent poultry; and 10 percent game birds. Vegetable matter, carrion, and other minor items were identified with most stomachs having combinations of many foods. The gray fox diet study proved similar, but it contained more vegetable matter.

Coyotes

Coyotes were not common, but their numbers have since increased statewide. They were called wolves, although the timber wolf had disappeared from Indiana many years earlier. Coyotes cross bred with dogs, and it was necessary to have skulls examined by the U.S. Biological Survey for true verification of this species.

Other Furbearers

Raccoon populations were low in the 1930s compared to the increase after 1940. Night hunters were lucky if their dogs treed a few during the two-month open season. Lack of a good distribution of water in the project area was a limiting factor, but Lake Greenwood and the creation of water holes helped alleviate this situation. In the spring of 1938, the Division of Fish and Game delivered five, pen-raised raccoons from the Wells County Game Farm. They were ear-tagged and released on the north side of the lake. We questioned their ability to survive in the wild when we discovered it was necessary to goad them to climb trees. After release, no reports were ever received.

Opossums have never been a favorite of hunters or trappers. They are the only marsupial found in this state. Skunks were present. I recall one that was wandering in the rubble of the foundation of a barn that had been torn down. It could have had a den there. Weasel and mink numbers were limited. The distribution of the latter was affected by the general lack of a good system of running streams. One old-timer told me that his dog trailed mink to their dens. The muskrat population was of no significance due to the lack of good aquatic habitat before Lake Greenwood.

Hunting and trapping of all furbearers contributed to the income of some residents. Many either shipped their furs or took them to a fur market on the courthouse square in Spencer. Statewide average prices paid for pelts in Indiana in 1937 were muskrat $.98, mink $6.72, raccoon $2.00, opossum $.27, skunk $1.00, weasel $.34, red fox $7.00, and gray fox $1.84. There was no record of badgers in the area. Some families also ate raccoon and an occasional opossum.

Predator Control

In the 1930s, the science of wildlife management was in the barbershop conversation stage. The Indiana Department of Conservation, Division of Fish and Game as well as other state and federal agencies emphasized control of predatory mammals and birds. Farmers felt that the loss of poultry, due to foxes, weasels, and other predators was a problem. Sportsmen felt that predation by foxes and other predators greatly reduced populations of some species.

In keeping with the general philosophy at that time, the control of red and gray foxes received far greater attention than control of birds of prey. In fact, control of the latter was of minor consequence. Fox populations over the entire state were high. Conservation clubs organized fox drives for sportsmen and landowners. These drives were mainly conducted on farmland. A section of land with roads on all four sides provided an ideal situation where lines of participants could start and converge in the center. As the area became smaller, persons with guns had to take precautions as a safety measure for others on the lines. Due to the terrain and more wooded portions of the project, these drives were not made there.

The federal government, through its U.S. Biological Survey, employed a predator control agent at Lafayette, Indiana. The agent, Mr. Oderkirk, gave assistance in the control of large numbers of pigeons and other birds in cities, as well as helping to stem damage to agricultural crops caused by large flocks of birds. Farmers complained about woodchucks digging holes under farm buildings or in fields where horses and cattle could break their legs. Oderkirk visited the project to advise on the control of foxes by using the same methods for eliminating woodchucks. A powder containing cyanide was placed in the entrance of a ground den. After plugging all holes, moisture caused the powder to emit poisonous fumes that killed any occupant foxes, but also skunks, woodchucks, and other forms of wildlife.

Rama Dye, a local worker, was assigned the task of controlling predators. I advised him to be very careful, as the fumes were also lethal to humans. Dye examined many dens to determine use. An entrance hole with spider webs or leaves showed no cur-

Outdoor Indiana, February 1934

OUTDOOR INDIANA
February 1934

Pokagon State Park

Starting with this first issue in February 1934, *Outdoor Indiana* promoted the activities of the divisions of the Department of Conservation.

rent occupancy. An active fox den often had fresh earth scattered around a clean entrance hole and other nearby evidence, such as fox tracks, hair, and other signs. Many woodchuck burrows contained several holes. Vixens usually used one of them during their breeding and rearing seasons in winter and spring. Despite all precautions to protect other animals, this was a poor method of predator control.

Indiana did not pay a state bounty on predators, but left it to each county. In Martin County it was necessary for a person to present evidence at the courthouse before payment. The usual procedure required the exhibit of the animal or its two ears. Coyotes, or so-called wolves, had to be verified by presenting the dead animal. No doubt, many were crosses with feral dogs. State biologists later investigated the connection between the amount of bounty system payments and the control of the annual populations of predators and found no connections. There were periods in which the numbers of these animals would be high, followed by low periods. The payment of bounties was a waste of taxpayers' money. Other small game numbers also fluctuated regardless of such payments or other control measures.

Predators generally ate what they could find, but some food items were highly preferred. Cattle, swine, and other domesticated animals were consumed as carrion. In any predator-prey relationship, prey must outnumber predators; for example, there must be fewer foxes than rabbits and mice. For some predators, such as coyotes, there was little information about feeding habits, but it was thought that they would be similar to the feeding habit of foxes.

Indiana law listed a few birds that were not protected. These included the great horned owl, goshawk, Cooper's hawk, sharp-shinned hawk, crow, and English house sparrow. The European starling, which had been introduced, had not reached a significant number in Martin County, and pigeons were not serious problems in small towns. Otherwise, game and certain migratory birds were protected by closed seasons, except during specified hunting periods in the fall and early winter. All other non-game species were protected year around.

In this discussion of unprotected, and protected birds of prey, anecdotal information is revealing. The great horned owl received its name because of its prominent ear tuft feathers. Like all forms of wildlife, it subsisted on a wide range of prey species. Pellets of regurgitated bones and hair were found under their roosts. I remember a report by Everett Inman about an owl that entered an open window in his chicken house and killed several of his chickens. Upon hearing the commotion, Inman closed the window and eliminated the intruder. This bird was a woodland inhabitant, and I always had a feeling of respect when hearing its low call of five hoots, especially on cold winter nights, when our family lived in the house built for the custodian at the boat house.

The goshawk, Cooper's hawk, and sharp-shinned hawk were all accipiters that flew with rapid wing beats. Their flights were usually low and direct from seclusion in trees or other hiding places. The goshawk was a winter migrant from the north. Regardless of its food preferences, it merited protection because of its infrequent occurrences and insignificant effect on wildlife. Cooper's hawks usually capture some birds. On a quail hunt in Perry County, a covey had scattered in a sassafras thicket. While trying to flush a single, a Cooper's hawk buzzed past me, but was unable to flush any birds in the thick cover. The smaller sharp-shinned hawk captures a higher percentage of songbirds than other species in the state.

Laws protected all other hawks and owls. Red-tailed hawks were common residents of the woodlands in the project area. I remember an incident when I was in the fire tower and saw one soaring above it. Suddenly, it made a direct dive attack on a hen in Everett Inman's chicken yard, but was unable to kill its quarry. Red-tailed hawks catch an occasional squirrel, chipmunk, or chicken, but far more mice and other items.

Red-shouldered hawks also fed on rodents along with frogs and snakes. They were infrequent in the area due to the absence of large lowlands, but their numbers should increase in the future around Lake Greenwood. An occasional harrier or marsh hawk could be seen coursing over open fields in search of rodents. However, they were more frequent outside the project area on more open farmland.

The sparrow hawk, or Kestrel, was quite common around farmland. This little falcon could be seen in the vicinity of buildings. They hovered over fields and perched on utility lines. From these elevations, they could see insects and mice on the ground. An occasional small bird entered their diet. On one occasion, when I was driving my car, I noted one flying across the road. When it dropped an object from its talons, I was surprised to find it to be a rufous-sided towhee, a bird of similar size.

During the 1930s, there was little regard shown for all hawks. In fact, the protected large buteos were all called "chicken hawks." Buteos had broad wings and broad tails. The native red-tailed hawk, red-shouldered hawk, and the rough-legged hawk, which came down from its northern breeding grounds, were the ones that usually fell to the gun. Their habits of sitting on poles or in open trees caused them to be targets for high-powered rifles. Their bodies could be seen hanging on wire fences along roads over the state. All predators had seasonal diets that varied somewhat, but each had definite preferences when their favorite prey was available. Many persons in the outdoors tend to remember incidents where predators have been seen pursuing or capturing beneficial prey species. These sightings do not necessarily represent their major feeding habits.

It should also be understood that the laws and practices used by the old Division of Fish and Game during the 1930s have gone through many changes and actually been reversed in some cases during ensuing years. Fish hatchery uses, stocking ratios, open seasons, and possession limits are some examples. Likewise, wildlife management has been altered by research studies. Artificial propagation of game birds and raccoons has been terminated. Habitat losses for small farmland game, like bobwhite quail, ring-necked pheasants and cottontail rabbits, have caused reductions in possession limits and other hunting regulations. Food habit studies of red and gray foxes, hawks, and owls have shown then to be beneficial. Hunting and trapping regulations now apply to foxes; and hawks and owls are now protected. Termination of the wasteful county bounty system has also helped.

The reintroduction of the white-tailed deer and wild turkey has greatly enhanced woodland game hunting, along with establishing a hunting season for ruffed grouse. The present forest acreage in the state is similar to the 1930s, and it has maintained the habitat for gray and fox squirrels during this long period. The research and regulatory considerations of that period have led to the modern management of fish and wildlife resources of today.

In summary, actions taken during the entire project development period in the management of the forest, fish and wildlife resources involved many interesting measures. Lake Greenwood created a higher biological diversity, and it made a major contribution to sportsmen, boaters, and the general public in southwestern Indiana. In addition to being the largest artificial impoundment in Southern Indiana, Lake Greenwood was located in the largest state forest. The combination of aquatic and terrestrial habitats for different kinds of wildlife also made an area for both hunters and other observers. If the area had not been retaken by the national government in 1940 and become part of Crane Naval Ammunition Depot, it could have maintained these diverse uses for a long period. As condemnation was not involved, the fragmented ownership of public and private land would have maintained farming practices adjoining woodlands and would have led to a slower decline in rabbit and quail populations. Most state forests still have private land ownership within their boundaries (in-holdings) more than fifty years after establishment. However, I believe that game and nongame species associated with the forested landscape would have eventually assumed dominance and benefited from the reversion of submarginal farmland to its original and better use. All these functions were, of course, altered when the use of the area changed in 1940. At that time the federal government retained landownership but gave the state a 99-year lease. The lease was revoked when the project area became the location of the Crane Naval Ammunition Depot.

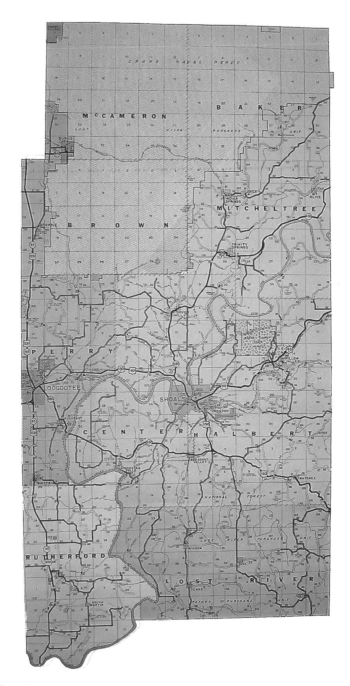

A map of Martin County in 1990 graphically illustrates the importance of Crane in the area. Size of original map 33^{15}/$_{16}$" x 16^{13}/$_{16}$"

PROJECT CLOSURE AND CRANE NAVAL AMMUNITION DEPOT

Our office had heard rumors about the termination of the project. In April, an official notice advised about the final date of June 30, 1940. Therefore, it became necessary for administrative personnel to seek other employment. I found that my interests had gradually changed from forestry to wildlife conservation, and I accepted a position with the Indiana Department of Conservation, Division of Fish and Game on July 1, 1940. I was appointed as Project Leader of Statewide Wildlife Survey and Demonstration Project 2R. This research project also involved individual studies of important small game and furbearing species.

The closure of the project had been brought about by national events. After the fall of France to Germany and the retreat of Great Britain at Dunkirk, the United States became more involved with the situation in Europe. As German submarine warfare had intensified, it gradually became evident that the United States should find a location away from its coastal regions to store naval ammunition. By early 1940, it was recognized that a large area with a lake existed in Indiana. Organizations and politicians began to lobby for the cancellation of the 99-year lease for a state forest and for the establishment of a naval ammunition depot in Martin County. The Indiana Department of Conservation regretted the loss of the area, but realized its great importance for the defense of our country. Thus, the "long-term" lease existed for only a few months. Congress' initial appropriation of $3 million for the establishment of the facility provided for acquisition along with construction contracts and plans. The Naval Ammunition Depot, Burns City, Indiana, was commissioned in December 1941.

The exact number of acres involved in the transfer back to the federal government is not clear. It was estimated to be around 32,000 acres. The state's figure was 32,971. This difference was mainly due to the location of the depot's south property line in Baker Township. It did not extend to the line between Baker and Mitcheltree townships. This excluded some of the tracts purchased by the U.S. Department of Agriculture for the Resettlement Administration Project. This land reverted to the Hoosier National Forest, which had been established in 1935. At a later date, an agreement between the federal and state governments established boundaries in south-central Indiana where areas could be purchased for federal or state forests. An exchange of land in this part of Martin County then transferred ownership back to the state, and it became part of Martin State Forest, which had been established in 1931. Surplus tracts in McCameron, Brown, and Perry townships were sold at public auctions. After land acquisition was completed, Crane contained 62,609 acres.

The acquisition of properties not previously purchased by the U.S. Department of Agriculture became imperative. The remaining landowners, who accepted the new federal appraisals, were given notice to vacate within a few days. Others, not agreeing with the offer, were also served the same notice and advised about settlement in court. Expenditures for acquisition were higher than usual. An average of $20.75 per acre was paid for land and improvements. This contrasted with the highest amount of $21.70 received by one landowner during acquisition for the Martin County project by the U.S. Department of Agriculture.

The availability of this large area with one-half of its land under public ownership made it possible to initiate immediate development of the ammunition depot. The Russell B. Moore Engineering Company won the bid to prepare plans for buildings and other facilities. Likewise, the Maxon Construction Company performed major construction work along with minor contractors. Storage magazines for high explosives were to be scattered over the base. Construction of buildings for assembling weapons, housing for officers and enlisted personnel, railroads and roads for transportation and surveillance, and many other supporting facilities were future tasks. Lieutenant Commander Wallace B. Short supervised construction and acquisition during the first nineteen months. Construction continued during the entire war period.

The administration and supervision of all operations at Crane were directly under Captain Edgar G. Oberlin. Naval officers under his command directed and inspected contractual work and trained supervising civilian personnel, including instruction in methods for the safe handling of high explosives. There were also many supporting facilities, such as housing for civilians at Crane Village. Lake Greenwood provided water for human consumption, sewage disposal, fire suppression, and all other needs. Marines patrolled miles of perimeter fences on horses and mules and manned entrance gates. Thus, Crane became a major support base for the U.S. Navy during World War II.

After the war ended in 1945, Crane remained open. Security and maintenance of storage magazines, scattered in groups over the base, continued. Like other military areas, Crane contained many types of surplus equipment and warfare materials. Free disposal was offered to different federal departments, followed by similar state agencies. The Indiana Divisions of Forestry and Fish and Game obtained trucks, tractors, and other heavy equipment used for construction and transportation purposes. The U.S. General Services Administration conducted public sales of remaining surplus items at designated locations in the state. It also notified and authorized the pick up of surplus by federal and state agencies.

At first, the tree planting program continued at Crane Naval Ammunition Depot; Works Progress Administration crews planted 250,000 trees each year until the program was terminated. During the ensuing years, sporadic planting continued. White, red, Virginia, and shortleaf pines were planted mainly along highways, borrow pits, and the burning field for ammunition disposal. The end of World War II permitted more time to devote to these important measures. This program is currently administered by personnel attached to the Plans and Specifications Branch of the engineering department in the Public Works Directorates. The program now includes a forest management section, soil and water conservation land management section, fish and wildlife section, and cultural resources plan.

When the 99-year lease between the federal and state governments was cancelled, less emphasis was placed on the management of the natural resources at Crane. Crane's primary mission was military functions, not the managment of natural resources. Buildings, storage facilities, highways, railroads, and other installations necessary for a major ammunition depot were constructed, and the work camp and most of the other buildings of the Resettlement Administration were dismantled, with the exception of those in the public use area, mule barn and house at the dam.

Some areas with tree plantations, timber stand improvement, water holes, and wildlife cover were destroyed, while others remained untouched. No doubt, the clearing and movement of soil by heavy equipment contributed to some siltation in Lake Greenwood. After the war, more attention was given to the natural resources. It is also of interest that the U.S. Navy hired a trained forester in 1941. Jack Frederick served from 1941 to 1951.

Crane Division, Naval Surface Warfare Center

Sporadic tree planting continued at Crane into the early 1970s. Crane now has one of the largest blocks of contiguous forested areas in Indiana. Its timber resources have gradually increased over the years and will continue to become greater in the future. Timber sales that were made from 1960 through 1991 showed a total volume of 15.7 million board feet of saw timber, along with other wood products such as pulpwood, poles and posts.

The area continues to serve as a place for study and recreation. The Purdue University Department of Forestry and Natural Resources conducts wildlife research

This picture, taken in 1955, shows white and red pines that were planted by the Resettlement Administration in the 1930s.

on Crane land. The Division of Fish and Wildlife, Department of Natural Resources stocked some fish and conducted fishery studies working with the U.S. Fish and Wildlife Service. Cultural and historical surveys have been conducted at Crane to identify archaeological and historical resources. Indiana University graduate students also find this protected environment to be ideal for studies of snakes, snails, and turtles. Another cooperative agreement involved the National Park Service regarding outdoor recreation.

In 1967, the Indiana Nature Preserves Act created the Division of Nature Preserves for the purpose of locating and protecting areas with unusual flora or fauna or with biotic, geological, scenic, or paleontological features. The large acreage at Crane, with its many topographic features, offered an opportunity to examine its natural communities. Fifty acres scattered over the entire base were selected for this inventory that resulted in a list of 216 vascular plants, including trees, shrubs, flowers, and ferns. The study included a search for rare and endangered plants. Rare plants are classified as those known on only one to five extant sites. The search at Crane revealed two rare plants, the single-head pussytoes and running club moss.

In 1993, the Chief of Naval Materials chose Crane as a source for white oak to repair the U.S.S. *Constitution*, a frigate built in 1794. The site (dubbed The Constitution Oak Groves) provided sixty trees for logs to repair the frigate, which is docked in Boston Harbor. Another supply will be needed in 2013 and in 2044 for replanking work on the ship; two stands have been reserved for growing large, high-quality white oak for this purpose.

When the U.S. Navy assumed jurisdiction of the area, the same six-mile foot trail that followed the south shoreline between Lake Greenwood dam and a point near former State Highway 45 was retained. Captain Steve Howard initiated a new interest in the hiking trail in 1993. Since that time a sixteen-mile foot trail for hikers and bird and wildlife watchers allows them to traverse the hills and valleys of this beautiful center. The trail, constructed by volunteer labor, has gradients that vary from gentle to steep. There are several spots where hikers can begin or terminate their walks around all sides of Lake Greenwood.

The 800-acre Lake Greenwood and adjoining 90-acre public use area are an important focal point for renewed recreational activity at Crane. A modern campground has sixty trailer sites as well as primitive campsites. Annual uses of the base for related outdoor recreation activities are estimated at 55,200, including

32,980 by the general public and 23,400 by Crane employees. Open House, a one-day event, attracts as many as 8,000 people, who learn about the purposes and functions of this base and view its operations.

The decision to acquire and convert this submarginal farmland to public use as a state forest and its subsequent transfer back to the federal government was an important action. During World War II, this inland area became a key naval center for the storage of ammunition and production of weapons. During and after the Cold War, Crane continued to contribute to the national defense of our country. New research and technology have greatly increased its mission. The U.S. Department of Navy's present designation is Crane Division, Naval Surface Warfare Center. Crane, a major producer of naval ammunition, has provided not only for naval and army forces, but also the marine corps, air force, and coast guard. Several thousand persons have been employed there each year. This facility has proven to be most fortunate for Martin County and surrounding counties. In fact, Martin County, as one of the poorest counties in the state, gained significant advantages.

Crane, the third largest naval base in the nation, is the second largest employer in southern Indiana and the twelfth largest in the state; nearly 4,000 people work there. However, Crane's influence reaches beyond just the number of people employed at the facility; each day Crane spends $1.3 million in Indiana. In addition, Crane partners with local industry, colleges, universities, and state government on projects. Since its transfer to federal ownership in 1941, Crane has been truly vital to the economy of southern Indiana.

EDITORIAL NOTE: There has been much anxiety about the fate of Crane as part of the 2005 Base Realignment and Closure (BRAC) process. As we go to press, Crane Division, Naval Surface Warfare Center, has apparently been saved from closure. The Pentagon in its Friday, May 13, 2005 announcement recommended that Crane remain open with a loss of close to 700 jobs. Indiana will try to save those jobs and increase jobs through partnerships with the private sector, universities, and other entities. Pentagon recommendations must be reviewed by the independent BRAC commission. The commission's recommendations must then be considered by the President and the Congress following a process with set deadlines for action.

Major coverage of the Pentagon announcement and its impact is available in the Indianapolis *Star*, May 14, 15, 2005 and in the following newspapers in areas especially relevant to this book: Bedford *Times-Mail*, May 13, 2005 and *Sunday Times-Mail*, May 15, 2005; Bloomington *Herald-Times*, May 14, 2005.

WORKS CITED

Books and Monographs

Allen, John M. *Gray and Fox Squirrel Management in Indiana.* Indiana Department of Conservation, Division of Fish and Game, Pittman-Robertson Wildlife Restoration Bulletin 1. Indianapolis: Indiana Department of Conservation, 1952.

Committee on *Forest Cover Types of North America.* Washington, D.C.: Society of American Foresters, 1967.

Deam, Charles C. *Flora of Indiana.* Indianapolis: Indiana Department of Conservation, 1940.

_____. *Trees of Indiana.* 3d ed. Indianapolis: Indiana Department of Conservation, 1953.

Holt, Harry Q. *History of Martin County Indiana.* Paoli, Ind., 1953.

Hughes, J. A. *Farm Game Habitat Restoration.* Indiana Department of Conservation, Division of Fish and Game, Pittman-Robertson Wildlife Restoration, 1935–1955, Bulletin 3. Indianapolis: Indiana Department of Conservation, 1955.

Jackson, Marion T., ed. *The Natural Heritage of Indiana.* Bloomington, Ind.: Indiana University Press, 1997.

Lindsey, Alton A., V. Schmelz, and Stanley A. Nichols. *Natural Areas in Indiana and their Preservation.* West Lafayette, Ind.: Purdue University, Department of Biological Science, 1969.

Lindsey, Alton A., ed. *Natural Features of Indiana.* Indianapolis: Indiana Academy of Science, 1966.

Madison, James H. *Indiana through Tradition and Change.* Indianapolis: Indiana Historical Society, 1982.

McElrath, George, Jr. *Soil Survey of Martin County, Indiana.* Washington, D.C.: U.S. Conservation Service, 1988.

Riker, Dorothy, comp. *The Hoosier Training Ground: A History of Army and Navy Training Centers…Within the State Boundaries During World War II.* Bloomington: Indiana War History Commission, 1952.

Reid, Robert L., and Thomas E. Rodgers. *A Good Neighbor: The First Fifty Years at Crane.* Evansville, Ind.: University of Southern Indiana, 1991.

Reid, Robert L. *Back Home Again: Indiana in the Farm Security Administration Photographs, 1935–1943.* Bloomington, Ind.: Indiana University Press, 1987.

Articles

Adams, William R. "Archaeological Survey of Martin County." *Indiana History Bulletin*, vol. 23, no. 6 (1946): 195–226.

Anderson, Robert, and Robert Ball. "Musseling In." *Outdoor Indiana* (July/August 1993), 42–49.

Barnes, William B., "The Distribution of Indiana's Bobwhite Quail." *Outdoor Indiana* (October 1947), 3–5.

_____. "The White-Tailed Deer in Indiana." *Outdoor Indiana* (March 1945), 4–5.

Kase, J. C. "Foxes Must Eat Too." *Outdoor Indiana* (June 1946), 14–15.

Mumford, R. E. "Ruffed Grouse." Pittman-Robertson Project W-2-R Indiana Department of Conservation, Division of Fish and Game. Indianapolis: Department of Conservation, 1954, 181–89.

"Land Use Area in Martin County is Dedicated—Covers 32,000 Acres." *Outdoor Indiana* (November 1939), 10–11, 22.

Thompson, Rebecca J. "Deshee Farm, A New Deal Experiment with Cooperative Farming." *Indiana Magazine of History* (Fall 1995): 380–406.

Unpublished Material

Poynter, David, Jr. "The History of the Forest of Crane Naval Weapons Support Center, Crane, Indiana." Unpublished Report, 1988.

State Government Publications

Indiana *Year Book*, 1940.

Indiana *Year Book*, 1943.

INDEX

Boldface page numbers refer to images.

A

Adams, William R., 6, 132

Akester, Robert, 25

Allee, Herbert, 59

American Legion, 18

Arnold, John, 54

Arvin, Thomas, 67

Ash, 6, 10, 43–45, 81–83, 86–88

Ash, Clarence, 61

Atlantic flyway, 109

Avoca State Fish Hatchery, 98

B

Baker, Allan, 5

Baker, Mildred, 64

Baker, Otway, 68

Baker Township, 33–35, 38, 49, 51, 63, 101, 126

Baker, Wilson, 63

Barnes, Cecilia Doyle, x, xvi, xiv, 64, **65**, 66, **78**

Z